The
Earth
Abides

Betty Taylor

Shapato Publishing
Everly, Iowa

Published by: Shapato Publishing
PO Box 476
Everly, IA 51338

ISBN: 978-0-9821058-9-4

Library of Congress Control Number: 2010926042
Copyright © 2010 Betty Taylor

First Printing June 2010

Cover and interior art provided by LaVonne M. Hansen
Photograph on back cover by Clayton Pyle

I dedicate this book to the memory of Anna Elizabeth Eckhoff Hembd, my paternal grandmother. She was born at sea, en route from Germany to America, on November 11, 1853. She and my grandfather raised their family on wooded Minnesota land about seventeen miles from LaCrosse, Wisconsin where they farmed and sold oak and birch wood in the late 1800s. A mother of nineteen, she instilled an enduring heritage of faith and love in her family, while finding time to write some poetry. Although she died twenty-two years before my birth, I sense a mystical connection to that remarkable woman, as do many of my siblings and cousins. This book is a generational recognition of my roots, with special admiration for Anna Elizabeth Hembd from her youngest granddaughter, Betty Anne Hembd Taylor.

LaVonne Hansen, award winning artist and retired bank teller, lives with her husband, Don, in Hartley, Iowa. LaVonne is noted in the surrounding area for delivering positive messages through her "chalk talks." While speaking, she illustrates her thoughts through appealing chalk drawings on 24" x 40" sheets. For ten consecutive years LaVonne donated local historical sketches to be auctioned off at Hartley's Threshing Days plus one more sketch for the quasquicentennial celebration. A few of her other achievements are illustrating calendars for a neighboring town and entering the art category at the Clay County Fair. Her pen-and-ink drawings appear in the memoir *Climbing—One Pole at a Time* by Irvin Goodon, as well as two other books by Shapato Publishing, *Walking Beans Wasn't Something You Did With Your Dog*, and *Knee High by the Fourth of July*.

ACKNOWLEDGMENTS:

Putting one's work together into a book is rather daunting. I would never have found the courage to take the risk, except for three interactions over a period of years. Twenty years may have passed since LaVonne Hansen first suggested that I put a collection of my poems together into a book, which she would illustrate for me. I smiled at the thought, but set it aside until LaVonne would bring it up again.

Then about a year ago Jean Tennant suggested that if I would put a collection of my poems together, Shapato Publishing would print it. LaVonne's offer came to my mind, but I still was not serious about the idea.

After my story was accepted for Shapato Publishing's first book, *Walking Beans Wasn't Something You Did With Your Dog*, Jean, LaVonne and I participated in several book signings along with other writers with stories in the book.

One of those events was in my hometown library in Ocheyedan, Iowa. My sister, Marjorie Brockshus, was in the audience. I mentioned that I once thought I would write a book, but I had never done that, and was privileged to have worked with Jean and to have a story in her book.

Marge interjected, "Well, you're not dead yet. There is still time."

That was my third nudge. I set out to compile this collection of poems and essays, chosen from my past twenty-plus years of writing. In addition, you will find a poem by my grandmother and an essay by her son, my father.

I owe a debt of gratitude to the members of writing groups in Spencer, Hartley, and Spirit Lake, plus two different writers' round robins. Members of those groups have provided me with valued comments, and I know my work has improved because of their help.

I've appreciated the editing advice from my good friend Susan Morphew, along with proofreading comments from Karen Schutt, Joe Hembd and Ellen Treimer.

It has been a privilege to have a frequent guest column in the Hartley Sentinel, providing me with an opportunity to make my work known in the area.

And then there is the group at MaeB's: especially Margaret Dau, Barb Haack and Lois Christensen. Writing is a lonely endeavor without encouragement from friends.

LaVonne Hansen's illustrations enhance the poems and stories, and I thank her for being so willing to discuss sketches with me and to see them through my eyes.

How can I say enough about Jean Tennant? I am only beginning to understand how inept my submission process has been. She is an excellent editor, coaches me on the computer, puts up with my tendency to change my mind, and has accepted and worked with a manuscript that no other editor would have bothered with.

And last, I thank my husband Orv for his comments, for seeing the humor in what I have written about our relationship, and for being a good sport about it. Without his encouragement and willingness to do a good share of the cooking and housework I would never have found the time to write.

Betty Taylor
Hartley, Iowa

FOREWORD

When Betty Taylor asked me to write the foreword to her new book, *The Earth Abides*, my first reaction was, "Sure, I can do that." Then, as I received the pages of her manuscript for formatting, panic began to set in. As I've often told Betty, "I don't know poetry." How was I going to write a foreword for a book of poetry?

But what I found within these pages is a collection of poems and essays that spoke to me, the reader, in a way much deeper than I'd expected.

Even the poetry.

The strength of *The Earth Abides* lies in its character studies. The essay "A Glitch in Time" is a humorous reminder that time marches on for all of us, and sometimes all we can do is laugh about it, while "The World According to Garth" celebrates the quirky characters we all meet at one time or another. These humorous slices-of-life nicely counterbalance the more serious "Remembering Joe Green," which made my heart ache for the boy in one of the retired teacher's long-ago classes, and "Circle of Friends" is a reminder of the strength of friendship and the fragility of life.

Then there's "Light Amid Darkness," which tells of the author's struggles with bipolar disorder. Though we'd spoken of this before, Betty and I, seeing her words in print, the struggles she'd endured, the years of misdiagnoses, helped me better understand the shadowy world of mental illness. I'm astonished by her bravery, and wonder if I could be so forthcoming.

Of the poems, I found them to be endearing and poignant examples of tightly disciplined prose, many of them reflecting the author's famous sense of humor. From "Universal Pleasure"—extolling the bliss of line-dried clothes—to "Glacial Deposits in Iowa Soil"—done in haiku sequence—there's a richness of words to please any reader.

I applaud the talents of an author who so skillfully articulates life's ups and downs. The pages herein offered me a glimpse of writing so masterfully done that I had only to sit back and enjoy the ride, letting each page take me to places I felt privileged to visit.

Including the poetry.

Jean Tennant

CONTENTS

INTRODUCTION

There is a Time for Everything, and a Season for Every Activity Under Heaven*

The words of The Teacher have haunting and intriguing perspectives about the times and seasons of life. Poets, philoscphers, and songwriters often paraphrase his words as reminders of personal observations and experiences. I assume that most of us interject our private lives into the text.

Five years ago I completed my "threescore years and ten," the amount of time allotted according to the Psalmist.** I like to think I am in the autumn of my life, but perhaps it is already winter and I have not yet recognized it.

For the most part my stories and poems are true, although, especially in the humor section, I admit to a bit of literary license to make the pieces more entertaining. Those who experienced the years with me may have memories and interpretations that differ from mine. Events may be shared, but the impact on each individual is unique. The mind seems to selectively store, ignore, minimize, or augment bits of conversations, observations, and experiences.

Each life is a mosaic of events and perceptions. The first two sections of this book are mostly humor. I suppose that is typical of my approach to life, as I often use humor to mask or soften those deeper emotions of fear, regret, grief, and rue. Along with The Teacher, I believe those emotions are common for each of us, combinations that make us what we are.

* Ecclesiastes 3:1
**Psalm 90:10

A Time

To Laugh

Universal Pleasure

There is nothing in the universe
like fresh, clean, line-dried clothes
a comfort to the body
and a pleasure to the nose.

Pastor Milquetoast

His voice is barely audible
from "Dearly Beloved" to "Amen."
He was wired for two hundred twenty
but plugged into a hundred and ten.

Keep Your Chin Up

I should have risen high in life
from standing on the pile
of the muck and mire I rose above
as I faced life with a smile.

But it is not a firm foundation
and I think I'm sinking in.
Someone ought to rescue me
it's almost to my chin.

In the Company of Losers

I get a lot of old-people jokes in my email box lately. For some reason, they are beginning to seem more real than ludicrous. I have been told that, as senior citizens, we must laugh at ourselves or we won't have anything to laugh about.

My husband, Orv, used to tell the story of a fellow he knew who drove his car downtown one morning. Forgetting that he had driven, he walked home. When he saw that his car was missing, he called the police to report the car stolen.

Also, an elderly couple from his hometown called the police one day. They reported a burglary. Two fur coats were missing from a closet. Police investigated with no satisfactory outcome. A few weeks later the wife found the coats in another closet. Again she called the police to announce that the burglars must have developed guilt feelings, because they brought the coats back but put them into the wrong closet.

These stories help Orv and me maintain our good humor, as we become more forgetful and things get lost around our house. Whichever one of us can't find something is likely to announce that someone stole it—to which the other replies, "Don't worry, they'll probably bring it back."

An item that often disappears is my can of Pam. When clearing my counter space, I might absent-mindedly pick up the aerosol can and chuck it under the sink with cleaning supplies. So far, I have not taken it to the washroom to use for hair spray— and I hope to avoid that one.

Orv takes it all quite magnanimously, as he loses his share of items also, but on occasion he shakes his head and mutters, "You sure have a time."

At times while folding the laundry I'm short a sock or two. When Orv folds clothes, he's more practical than I am. He just puts a couple of mismatched socks together. I save the odd ones for a few weeks before I give up and throw them away, just before the mates appear in my laundry basket. One friend of mine wondered if her husband might throw single socks from the window while driving down the road just to torment her.

We sometimes work together framing pictures or putting finishing touches on antiques. Hammers hide. Glue gets lost. Phillips screwdrivers are the only ones in the rack when we need one for slotted screws. But if we need a Phillips—well, you guessed it—only straight screwdrivers are available.

One day I was looking for the Whiteout to correct an error on an envelope. It was nowhere to be found. Later, while looking for Scotch tape, I found the Whiteout. Now I can't find either one. Come to think of it, I believe I lost the envelope as well.

Orv is a creature of habit and always reads the newspaper with his breakfast. One morning while adding a couple of last-minute items for the garbage pick-up, I noticed that the paper had arrived. I thought I would do him a favor and bring it in while he was downstairs walking on his treadmill. When I went back into the house, I picked up the phone to make an early morning call. About ten minutes later he came upstairs and went out to get the paper. It wasn't there.

"Did you pick up the paper this morning?" he asked.

"Yes, didn't I put in on the kitchen table?"

It was nowhere to be found. Orv is not a patient person, but somehow he took that much better than I deserved.

"Did you look in the refrigerator?" he quipped.

I knew I hadn't put it there, but checked anyway. "Someone must have stolen it," I said lamely.

"Don't worry," he added, as he picked up the *Newsweek* magazine that came the day before. "They'll bring it back."

We went on about the morning, but from time to time throughout the day, I continued to hunt for that paper.

As evening approached, I needed to make another phone call. When I opened the drawer that holds the phone books, I found the morning paper. I guess the burglars did bring it back after all.

Remembering the Waterbed

Recently we faced decisions about buying a new bed. We could choose from a sleep number, a memory-foam top, firm mattress, pillow top—but you have seen the ads, you know that trying to make those decisions can go on and on.

I recall when firm beds were the order of the day for bad backs. Many years ago we bought one—king size. It almost filled the room. After sleeping on it for a week, I said, "Think of all the money this cost. We could have had the same level of comfort by tossing a blanket on the floor." We adjusted to it, but by the next time we went bed shopping, the recommendation was to buy one a bit less firm.

Of all the beds we ever owned, the waterbed was the most memorable. We loved the comfort and the constant temperature. In spite of its good points, it presented a bit of frustration. There was a slight difficulty in rolling over, which we adjusted to, but we never adjusted to dealing with the leaks. The routine was hook up a hose, shove it down the laundry chute, drain it into the basement shower, locate and patch the offending spot, refill the bed, set its thermostat, and hope it would be warm enough by bed time. We must have followed that routine a half dozen times or more during the years we owned it. Our friends had waterbeds with bladders that never leaked. I don't know why ours did. Maybe it had kidney stones.

One Saturday morning it seemed my toe was damp. I ignored the telltale signs and decided it was my imagination. Sunday the truth could not be denied. My whole foot was wet.

The previous year, while patching a leak, we vowed that we would never patch another. Still I searched for the offending spot, thinking that if it would be on top I might mend it just one more time. I weighed the advantages. It was always warm, it was always supportive, and contrary to one friend's fears, it did not cause us to drift apart.

The leak was not on top. With great effort I lifted the bladder in several places and found more water underneath, along with a faint smell of mildew. But I did not find the leak. I dried it as well as I could but Monday morning the bed was damp again.

"This is the last time," I sighed, "We're going to buy a new bed, the kind that never leaks."

Orv agreed and told me I could write a check on his account, but he would not help with the shopping. I thought that was fair enough. I know he hates to shop, so with check in hand I headed for the furniture store. The variety was not as great as it is today. I found green ones, blue ones, and pink ones. Some were four inches thick and some were eight, with varying levels of hardness. Some had handles for maneuvering and some did not. There were those on sale with rebates and those not on sale with no rebates. After careful study I chose an eight-inch mattress and box spring, to be delivered that very afternoon. I went home, attached the hose, shoved it down the clothes chute, and drained the leaky waterbed into the basement shower one last time.

That night we slept on our new mattress. We knew it would take some time to adjust, but the initial comparison was not on the side of the new bed. Orv had three comments: "It's easier to roll over, it's cold, and it feels like it has about 50 gallons too much water in it."

Love in the Woods

She was a sensuous maple tree
and he a sturdy oak.
Their limbs touched and they connected
long before they spoke.

They brushed against each other
from April to July.
He asked her pointed questions
she answered him with sighs.

"Squirrels planted me," quoth he.
"I was a nut in former days."
"My seeds were parachutes," she blushed.
"I had free un-rooted ways."

Birds and insects took up residence
children climbed their trunks and limbs.
He loved her with deep ardor
she felt the same for him.

In the fall she wore a crimson dress
 he had rustic, rusty leaves.
He thought she was quite fetching
swaying in the breeze.

It was winter that undressed them
left them bare and stark.
He found her quite attractive
stripped down to the bark.

Snow dressed her then in winter white
fitting for a bride
and he was such a handsome groom
standing by her side.

They never left each other
though lesser loves would fail.
They weathered every storm of life—
blizzards, rains, and hail.

Little seedlings grew around them
to fill their lives with laughter
so as it was in fairy tales
they were happy ever after.

My Diet Group

We hope to solve our problems
in our meeting room.
Our taste buds aren't just budding,
they've long been in full bloom.

Shape Up!!

Exercise, exercise
build up your stamina
stay out of the kitchen
don't eat that pie.

It's not nutritious, its
gastrointestinal
designed just to hasten
your time to die.

Going into Overtime

You may have heard of the book entitled, *Women are from Venus—Men are from Mars*. Once, when we still thought it was a planet, I told my husband he must be from Pluto because he's so far out. Rather than being insulted, he smiled, nodded, and seemed sort of proud of that.

Orv played baseball in high school. One of the highlights of his life came during his sophomore year. The year was 1939. The high school had about sixty students and the team had only ten uniforms, yet they qualified for the state tournament. They lost only one game that season, the final game of that tournament. Later Orv played baseball while in the Army. He was on his way to becoming part of the invasion of Japan when the atomic bombs were dropped. Instead of fighting a war, he served a tour of duty as part of the Occupation Forces. By accepting guard duty at night, he was free to be on the baseball team in the daytime. Following his discharge Orv played as an outfielder and relief pitcher in town team baseball for ten exciting seasons.

These days it is not unusual for him to spend evenings glued to the TV set during the baseball season. He shows greater interest in the ball games than in talking to me. That annoyed me in the early years of our marriage. Wherever we went, he seemed to find a ball game on the car radio, and would become engrossed even if the broadcast came from a distance and the static was horrible.

I'm a person who likes to visit, but when I hear Orv's dry comment, "My ears are getting tired," I know it's time for me to find something else to do, look for someone else to visit with, or to just be quiet.

With passing years we found ways to cope with his preoccupation with baseball and my lack of interest in the sport. He keeps the volume low on the TV set, while I might read or work crossword puzzles. At various times when I had more energy, I sewed, caned chair seats, or framed pictures. During my teaching career, I checked papers. Now I enjoy conversations with friends and family by telephone and e-mail, or read books and scan newspapers on line. I vaguely hear him cheer or complain loudly about plays, players or coaches, as if someone were really listening to him.

A few years ago we scheduled an October trip to a favorite spot in Ontario. The leaves were breathtaking in shades of reds, browns and gold, the weather was great, and everything was just right—except the World Series was on. To me, the logical thing was to turn the news on in the morning to see who had won the previous game, but Orv did not follow my logic. We were in a lovely condo with a kitchen, which gave us the privilege of cooking and washing dishes. There I was, without my computer or my hobbies, and there he was, glued to the TV set every evening. I vowed I would not travel with him again during the World Series.

Little did we know that the following year, instead of being on vacation, we would be in St. Mary's Hospital in Rochester, Minnesota, during the Play-Offs. Orv was about to have surgery for a rather large tumor located between the dura mater and the upper skull.

After a long day, filled with delays and frustrations, I waited anxiously as they wheeled him out of intensive care. They had removed a piece of the skull about three by four inches, replaced it with a product called *Norean,* and sewed the scalp back in place. I met him in the hall and we exchanged comments of relief over the fact that the tumor had been benign. As they put him in his bed, he looked up at the clock to see that is was after eight o'clock in the evening.

His next words were, "I missed the doggone ball game."

Other women seem to enjoy sports. Sometimes I listen in amazement while they discuss games with him. Even his seven-year-old great niece knows a lot about the players and teams. We had a neighbor woman who at age ninety-two could discuss sports with him intelligently, in spite of being legally blind. So why can't I enjoy them? I made feeble attempts through the years to care, but finally concluded that it was never going to happen. After many years we've learned to accept each other as we are, alike in many ways but extremely different in others.

Still, I am always relieved when the baseball season is over. But the reader must not conclude that we have a lot of togetherness when it ends. Football starts before baseball ends, and basketball is in full swing before the Play-Offs are over.

Not too long ago, I was lying on the couch re-reading *Women Who Run with the Wolves.* As I finished the chapter about the meaning of the Bluebeard myth, I looked up to notice that he was watching reruns of a boxing match. Mohammed Ali was dancing around George Foreman.

"I thought he had Parkinson's," I quipped. "How come he's boxing again?"

Orv didn't say a word, but gave me a look. I knew just what he was thinking. His ears were getting tired.

Of Genealogy and Outhouses

Our extended family is unique in more ways than one. About three years ago a cousin made an interesting suggestion. "Why don't we start a family email correspondence? When we receive an email, we can hit 'reply all' and get into an immediate discussion with everyone."

The idea was met with enthusiasm and when word of our correspondence got around, our numbers began to grow. Cousin Russ has a good sense of humor and a fascination with words, so when our numbers swelled to twelve, he informed us that we had become a dodecagon. We have since more than doubled the number of twelve, but since Russ hasn't come up with a new name, I just call it "the cousins' email."

We exchange open discussions about a variety of things. Many in the group have a gift for rhyme so we might all pitch in with inane rhyming birthday or get-well greetings. If illnesses are severe we exchange prayers and sympathetic thoughts. We express concern for those dealing with an overabundance of snow or too much rain and wonder how everyone is coping in these times of economic crisis. Political discussions get a bit sticky at times, so we try to be careful with them.

Our cousin, Don, is the genealogist of the group. He researched our family name, Hembd, and found it was once Von Hembd in Germany. He located a related branch by the name of Hemptine who once owned a castle in Belgium. That news was too good to let pass, so we invented royal names for ourselves. For a while I went by Queen Bess, the name of a silverware pattern I once purchased with Betty Crocker coupons. Later, since we all like to write rhyme—and to honor my town of Hartley, Iowa—I changed my signature to "Betty the Bard of Hartley."

Email-loving participants live east as far as Illinois, west to New Mexico and Washington State, south to Texas, and for a time, a distant cousin I have yet to meet, sent messages while she was serving with the military in Iraq.

My nephew, Joe, lives alternately in Sioux City, Iowa or at Benson's Landing on the Missouri River near Vermillion, South Dakota. Joe calls himself Chief Joseph of the Sioux or Chief Joseph on the Mighty Missouri, depending on where he is at a given moment. He has a modern home with good plumbing on his river-front property, but it occurred to him that, for the sake of convenience and perhaps charm, the place should also have an outhouse. Recently he posed a simple question on the cousin's email. "How deep should an outhouse hole be?" Needless to say, he did not get simple answers.

Don, the family genealogist from Kent, Washington chimed in first with the following:

Hi Joe:

How do I approach the outhouse subject? I suppose as far as city government is concerned, no permit would be issued for digging it, so the architect (That would be the digger) most likely can call his own shots. Back when we were kids the hole was dug until the digger got tired, then they called it OK.

A more important subject is, "How far should the toilet seat be off the floor?" Here again it is probably left to the discretion of the architect but one should keep in mind that, when sitting on the seat, the feet should be able to reach the floor. My friend in Alaska built an outhouse on his five acres in Soldotna and he didn't have a ruler with him. So he measured from the knees to the feet and used that distance to represent the toilet seat height. What he failed to factor in was, he is six feet, six inches tall. So when I went to use the facility, I almost needed a stepladder to get up to the seat. I guess what I'm trying to say is you are pretty much on your own.

Sir Don of Kent

Since I am among the senior members of the group, I presumed it would behoove me to offer a few sage comments befitting one who grew up using an outhouse:

Dear Joe,

I don't know about the depth of the hole—but I do remember Dad digging a new one once. I believe the most important thing is to quit digging before the hole becomes too deep to climb back out. Also Dad put powdered lime on the contents from time to time, causing them to shrink a bit so a given hole would last longer.

Our Aunt Freda always went a step farther than anyone else. She saved the round cut outs for the seats, put handles on them so they could cover the holes not in use, then painted the bench, lids and general insides of the toilet. Still in spite of her best efforts, her outhouse had the same distinctive odor as anyone else's.

If you want an authentic touch to your outhouse—forget the toilet paper. I have an outdated Penney's catalog you can have. Sears, Roebuck or Montgomery Wards were the preferred catalogs of our outhouse days, but I don't have one of those, so Penney's will have to do. And it's too bad you can't buy a lug or two of peaches wrapped individually in soft paper these days. Those papers were a relief from catalog paper with a touch that would rival Charmin.

For the final, just-right effect, saw a cutout above the door— one that looks like a quarter moon. Our outhouse on the farm did not have one, and I always thought it should. Also consider this word of caution. Don't sit out there with the door closed on Halloween, in case someone tips the outhouse over, because you will have one heck of a time getting out.

Betty the Bard of Hartley

Overwhelmed with gratitude for the good advice, Joe replied:

Dear Relatives,

Thanks for the feedback. After the first foot of roots and soil, we hit sugar sand and continued to dig that out until the last three or four feet, which turned out to be clay. I was worried that if we dug deeper we would either hit water or Mr. Chan. The seat is a porcelain fixture with no trap, just a cylinder with a base as wide as the top. It is designed for attaching a standard toilet seat. The outhouse next to our old cabin is a two-seater. I can't grasp the concept of a two-seater, as I can never recall saying to family or friend, "I am headed for the toilet, come and join me . . . it's a two-seater!" Perhaps back when it was built, it was already common practice for women to go to the public toilets in pairs! Anyway, we will get by just fine with a one-at-a-timer. I was going to make mine 4' x 3,' but added an extra foot to accommodate a bin for cobs . . . just in case.

Chief Joseph on the Missouri,
home of the homemade and
home-filled outhouses.

Joe's cousin, Roger, of Spirit Lake, Iowa had no advice, but added these explanatory bits of information:

Joe,

My wife, Rita, was born south of Ocheyedan, and didn't have modern plumbing until she moved into town in March of 1969. I, on the other hand, was born on the north side of Ocheyedan, five-plus years before Rita. I am a member of a litter of six siblings, born in less than eight years. I don't remember not having modern plumbing. We had a "three-holer" as a backup when the women of the house took too long in our one indoor toilet. (As a side note, my mother has the best-looking peonies you have ever seen on the spot where that old three-holer once stood). Anyhow, the reason for more than one hole, according to my knowledgeable wife, is so each person can have a seat that fits his or her backside (small, medium, large).
Well, that's enough toilet talk—it's time for supper.
Sir Roger of the Lakes,
home to lots of modern plumbing

After a few more exchanges about a gal named Loo and a guy named John, Joe reported that his project was finished. He sent pictures and invited us to come for the viewing. The invitation included an opportunity for down-river tubing, a bit of fishing, a cookout and evening bonfire. I can just imagine what yarns we could spin around that fire.

The Bearded Lady

Jenny the Bearded Lady
was the feature of the show.
She never had a sweetheart
but she had a lot of dough.

Then Jack the Loafer had a thought.
I'll wed Jenny though she's weird.
We could live off Jenny's earnings
get rich off Jenny's beard.

So he set out to woo and win her
to make her think that it was love.
She resisted him at first
but Cupid gave her heart a shove.

Then Jenny was embarrassed
about her bearded chin—
longed to be prettier for Jack
to be more feminine.

She shaved because she loved him
but too late poor Jenny learned
when your sweetheart is a loafer
A Jenny shaved is a Jenny spurned.

A Word to the Wise

Before we learned about self-esteem, damaging the psyche or being politically correct, we had words to live by, words we memorized and took to heart. Any situation could and did remind us of Bible verses; rhyming poems, which denoted truth and purity; or contemplative mottoes about God, country, Mom and apple pie. Parents, teachers and friends quoted valued phrases, designed to build character, teach discernment and enlighten future generations. Prudent advice was contained in such phrases as:

- If it's not one thing, it's another
- Haste makes waste
- Pride goes before the fall
- Practice makes perfect
- Make the best of it
- It could be worse
    and on and on and on.

My parents sought to discourage my constant chatter by reminding me that silence is golden or children should be seen and not heard.

Dad valued Bible passages in general and at times was known to dwell on the one that says, "Spare the rod and spoil the child." He gave voice to that passage quite a lot, but since I was the youngest of seven children, he was too tired to act on it much. Still he often speculated that my behavior might improve if he followed through more often.

"A penny saved is a penny earned" was a favored proverb for those who struggled to recover from the Great Depression, pay off mortgages, and save up for the next depression, which was surely approaching. Yes, the handwriting was on the wall! Sometimes my mother would nod her head and sagely remark, "There will come a time . . ." I was never sure what that meant, but I could see that it was grave, so opted not to ask.

I believe Mom made up axioms to suit her own purposes. She was known to say, "Waste not want not" but often added, "If we waste what the Lord has given us, sooner of later, he will take if from us."

So she darned socks, cut buttons from worn-out clothes and saved them in a button jar, patched overalls, and sometimes patched the patches on those overalls with fabric gleaned from the good parts of jeans to be thrown away.

Before the days of plastic bags, dry goods purchases were wrapped and tied. Every household had a ball of string saved from those packages. The brown wrapping paper could be used for drawing, to apply to backs of pictures or to line dresser drawers. Once my sister and I made brown-paper kites and decorated them with crayons. The project kept us out of trouble for a time, but the end result didn't look all that great and the kites were too heavy to fly. Wrapping paper from birthday and Christmas gifts was also treated carefully, set aside, and recycled for another time.

My mother had zillions of ways to save and I bought in to most of them, but I drew the line when she tried to teach me the value of paring apples with paper-thin peelings. Mom good-naturedly accused me of chopping the apples square when I peeled them. We had our own orchard, and I knew the apples wouldn't fall far from the trees, but I also knew they would indeed fall. Then we would have to gather them and throw them over the fence for the hogs. I remained unconvinced that my less than careful paring constituted a wasteful act.

Today with the rising cost of fruit, I can see that being able to leave paper-thin parings would be a good thing. I compensate for that unlearned skill by baking whole, unpeeled apples with a little butter and brown sugar. Apple pie is no better and baked apples are a lot less work.

During the war years when many things were rationed, a popular slogan was, "Fix it up, wear it out, make it do, or do without." My parents loved that one. Dad straightened and reused nails and mended all sorts of things with baling wire. He milked his cows, picked corn, and loaded manure by hand. Mom sewed our clothes and saved the remnants to make patchwork quilts while touting the virtues of making do. She used to comment that "Some women can spend more by the teaspoonful than their husbands can bring in by the shovelful."

Words of wisdom did not stop with economics. Mom warned me to be careful about choosing friends by saying, "One bad apple can spoil the whole barrel," or "Birds of a feather flock together."

When I objected to what others had done and thought a little revenge might be in order, she had another approach. She would admonish me by saying, "Do unto others as you would *have* them do unto you—not as they *did* unto you," or "Two wrongs don't make a right," and "Don't make mountains out of mole hills."

Then there was my German immigrant grandfather. He had some words of wisdom that never caught on with the general public. When he observed overly objectionable behavior, he would say, "Some people, *ven* they go *crrrazy*, they get in the *het* first."

Dad was known to moralize, but his sense of humor allowed him to add his own twist to proverbs with comments like, "The early bird catches the worm—but if the worm hadn't been out so early, he wouldn't have been caught," or "Where there is a Will, there is a Wilhelmina," that "Love is blind, but the neighbors ain't," or "Beauty may be skin deep, but girls really go for that skin!"

Truth resides in the axioms and proverbs, but not necessarily the whole truth and nothing but the truth. They can oversimplify and present a rather narrow view of life. Today, writers are encouraged to be careful with idioms and avoid them like the plague. As I am resurrecting a few of them, I am reminded that old sayings in some distant past were new and original. I once heard of a person who read Shakespeare for the first time. She commented, "I don't see why everyone thinks he was such a great writer. His work is just full of clichés."

The Bad Taste of Rubber

Telephones have definitely changed through the years. What would Alexander Graham Bell think of the phone's evolution since the day he called, "Watson, come here, I want you"?

For that matter, what would my father think? He used to tell stories about how inhibited people were when phones first appeared in homes and general stores. He witnessed one old German fellow who came into the store to call his wife with news that their son had arrived on the train after being gone for a long time.

When the operator connected him, he hollered, "*Yon iss* on the *vay* home." Then he hung up with no further ado and went about his business.

Old telephones with extended mouthpieces, cranks, bells, receivers on the side, generators on the inside, and a place for batteries, are collectible now. When the dial system evolved, hundreds of the old phones were happily trashed. The ones that survived that purging have become rather valuable. Variations are priced at two to three hundred dollars and more. Even the dial phones that followed are relics. The one in my basement fascinates young people, who are surprised that it actually works.

There was no phone in our house in my early years. My parents had survived doctor bills and the Depression era. Virtues like getting by, scrimping and saving, were almost as sacred as attending worship services on a regular basis. It was exciting when the Kellogg phone finally came to hang on our dining room wall. It seemed a great luxury and source of fascination. We could call the six neighbors on our party line by using a series of short and long rings for each house. If we wished to call the operator, we used just one ring. She could connect us with those on lines other than our own. Dad showed us how to turn the crank to make it ring.

"You can use the phone when necessary," he cautioned, "but don't talk too long, and there will be no rubbering in this household. It's bad manners."

Rubbering was a term used to describe listening to someone else's call. Dad's firmness made me feel that God would most likely give me a siege of the boils if I committed such an invasion of privacy.

The neighbors did not all have the same thoughts. Catching up on what was happening up and down our gravel road was commonplace. Most phone conversations were rather general, and personal matters were discussed face to face. Teen-age boys were likely go to a house to ask for dates rather than call on the phone, and the idea of a girl calling a boy was considered as tasteless as rubbering.

Our phone number was 8F3-5, indicating that we were on line eight and could be summoned by three short rings and one long one. Numbers one through four indicated the shorts, and five indicated a long. Turning the crank on our own phone activated rings in every home on the party line.

The telephone operator knew much of what was going on in the community and served the purpose of the 9-1-1 of that era. If a tragedy struck, she would give a general ring, which was one long continuous ring. Everyone would rush to the phones to hear what had happened and to learn where help was needed. We could also give a general ring on our own party line.

Not all of the neighbors had phones. One day two children from the next farm came running breathlessly down the road. "We need Mr. Hembd to come over," they gasped, "Alan fell in the well."

For one of the few times in his life, I saw Dad look insecure. I could see that he hated to load the ladder and get into the car. While I had my first experience at spontaneous prayer, my mother cranked out a general ring to announce the problem to the neighbors, and then she called the local doctor.

Alan's parents had dug a small well using a posthole auger, extending the handle until they reached water. The toddler of the family had slipped into it. Since the well was narrow he was not totally immersed, but was stuck part way down, up to his waist in water and just out of reach. The ladder was useless.

While my mother was looking worried, his mother was lying on the ground with a cane hooked under Alan's little arm, which had lifted over his head as he fell. Dad recounted later that the men decided to dig a ditch deep enough for someone to lie down, grasp the boy's hand, and pull him free. The digging caused dirt to fall onto his upturned face, and they had to quit. Someone suggested putting a bucket over the hole, but the darkness frightened the crying child.

Soon Dr. Thayer arrived. He was not the stereotypical country doctor. He was often seen in off-white pants, wing-tip shoes, shirt, tie and a blazer. He stood out among the farmers in their Osh-Kosh-B'Gosh bibbed overalls and blue chambray shirts.

When he saw the distraught mother, he paid no attention to his clothes, but knelt on the ground beside her to offer comfort and reassurance.

Dad suggested they start at the backside of the needed ditch, dig away from the hole, and pull the last bit of dirt away with their hands. He and two others quickly dug the ditch. Alan's father lay in it, grasped the little hand and pulled his son to safety. He was cold from being partly submerged and dirty from soil falling on his face, but he was alive and much relieved. The doctor checked him over, found him to be sound, prescribed that he be bathed, coddled, and put to bed to be warmed and recover from the shock.

But Alan didn't take to the coddling very well. He soon threw off his covers and announced, "I want something to eat."

Probably the parents and the neighbors took longer to recover from the shock than Alan did. The well was covered and life went on as usual.

When Germany agreed to unconditional surrender to end the war in Europe, a general ring brought the message and the good news. My oldest brother came home from World War II after being gone for four and a half years. He was rather good-looking and a bit sought after.

It didn't take long before he met the woman he would soon marry, but other women did not give up easily. Listening in to calls made by ringing three shorts and a long on line eight, became quite interesting. One night the phone rang about five times while we were enjoying our evening meal. The nerve of the women who called him annoyed my mother. The clicks on the line from rubbering neighbors annoyed my father.

Bob was just plain annoyed. He grabbed his cap, stomped toward the door, turned to Mom and groused, "Just say I'm not home."

Three shorts and a long was a source of neighborhood curiosity again a few years later. My sister had recently moved to Nebraska for her first teaching job. It was not long before she called to say that she was making wedding plans. As the calls became more frequent, the neighbors became more interested and couldn't resist picking up the phones to rubber. Too many lifted receivers weakened the signals and it became harder and harder for my parents and sister to hear each other. I watched Dad's growing frustration during one such conversation.

Finally he announced, "Maybe if all you rubber-necks would hang up, I could have a conversation with my daughter."

He heard a *click, click, click, click*, up and down the line, and the conversation resumed. No one argued much with Dad face-to-face, and it seemed they did not cross him on the party line either.

In 1956, when most of the country had switched to dial, I lived near May City, Iowa, a small community that still had a party line. Visitors found my relic of a telephone to be quite a source of amusement. As many of the people in the area were of German descent, my good friend, Doris, looked at my phone and quipped, "Does the operator speak English?"

Minnie did indeed speak English and was at times a great source of information. Once some out-of-town friends were in the area and decided to pay us an impromptu visit. They called the operator from a local gas station and gave our number so they could call us for directions to the house.

When Minnie heard the number they were calling, she commented, "Oh they aren't home today, but I can hook you up with the people they are visiting."

We never found out how she knew where we were, but she certainly provided a service that modern phones don't offer.

Our telephone system has advanced far beyond the humble beginnings of Bell's invention. Today we carry our phones around with us. At one time, the cell phone inhibited me as much as early telephones inhibited the old German fellow Dad used to chuckle about. Now I enjoy reaching my children, grandchildren, and friends at any time. There is no denying the value of cell phones for summoning help in times of crisis. In our global world, calling 9-1-1 far outranks the general ring.

Even though I've learned to take pictures on the little gadget, I don't believe that skill enhances my life very much. And as for learning to text and tweet, well, that's totally out of the question—so far.

With the passing of the party line one could assume that rubbering, an activity my father considered to be in bad taste, is gone forever. Well, maybe it's a thing of the past, or maybe in our times of advanced technology, it just operates under a new name—wire-tapping.

I do believe Alexander Graham Bell and Dad would be amazed.

Weather Jester

Spring was only teasing
with its breath so clean and sweet.
It gave us all the fever
to plant and make things neat.

We put away snow shovels
got garden tools together
set out our seeds and seedlings
in early March spring weather.

But morning light surprised us
as the winds began to blow
and garden tools were covered
with three inches of fresh snow.

Final Performance

She acted like she knew it all
when she was in school.
She acted like she loved him
then made him out to be a fool.

When she couldn't have her way
she acted like she cried.
So we buried her quite quickly
when she acted like she died.

A Time
to Gather

Obsessed

I can't stop buying antiques.
Auctions call me
garage sales beckon
eBay beguiles
and shops consume vacation time.

Collected treasures crowd us
from the family room
and cars from the garage.

May I spend my declining years
in a cane seated wheel chair
and ride to my final resting place
in a curtained, horse-drawn hearse.

A Glitch in Time

The day was hot. July in Iowa is always hot, but the July of 2001 was worse than ever. My husband and I were venturing on an eighty-mile, antiquing trip. We had sold a china cabinet, with an agreement to deliver, and planned to stop at various shops to see what bargains we might be able to buy for resale. Our conversations went from our destination and places we would patronize, to an increasing excitement about our upcoming fall road trip to Newfoundland.

Once Orv commented, "I'm going to get new tires on the van before we travel this fall."

He usually makes it a point to have good tires, and seldom needs to change one for us, but frequently we have stopped to help motorists in trouble. I often watched him quickly and efficiently change tires, especially for women or elderly people.

We arrived at the buyer's home about two minutes before the promised time. If I had been driving we might have been late, but as with his tires, Orv is careful with his time. Laboriously we unloaded the china cabinet. When I made the deal with a promise to deliver, I did not anticipate carrying the item to the basement. I'd had brain surgery the previous summer, and though I had regained my strength, my balance was a bit uncertain. I leaned heavily on the railings to steady myself as we negotiated the stairs and put the piece in place. I was a bit disgruntled, but the buyer was pleased, and we were on our way.

A pleasant sprinkle cut the summer heat and we studied the western sky, hoping that rain was refreshing our area. We made a few stops at familiar shops. We purchased a Red Riding Hood cookie jar, a parlor table, a coffee grinder, and several other items. A vendor in one of the antique malls invited us to look at garage sale items she had set out for the following weekend. There we purchased two quilts, a bean pot, and a parlor table. We left her garage in the midst of a downpour. Satisfied that we had spent enough money and most of my energy, we turned toward home.

I tossed my cane in the back of the van, relieved that we had not filled the van too full for me to recline. After a few moments, I loaded one of our books on tape. We had just begun to listen to Tom Brokaw's voice reading *The Greatest Generation* when we heard an unwelcome flopping sound. The van swayed just a bit and Orv pulled the car off the road. We had a flat tire.

As owners of our third Dodge Caravan, we knew the spare hung under the back part of the chassis, but that was all we knew about changing its tires that July afternoon. After checking around, Orv found a compartment on the back left side of the van. It held a jack, unlike any he had ever used. After some jabs at trial and error he figured out how to raise the van. He got under the car and set out to loosen the spare. One car after another sped by as I heard him mutter things under his breath about the eternal perdition of the van, the tire, and the jack. The thought crossed my mind that had I been alone, someone would have stopped and changed the tire for me.

I retrieved the instruction book from the glove compartment. As I leaned heavily on my cane, I read instructions and looked at diagrams. We soon learned that raising the vehicle was not necessary to release the spare. We simply needed to use the jack handle to turn a nut hidden under the carpet. That simple procedure lowered the tire to the ground. The release was easy. At last he freed the tire and took it to the front driver's side. Cars continued to speed by.

He moved the jack, but couldn't find a proper place to put it under the car. Once more I stood there, leaning on my cane, reading the instruction book while Orv, still muttering, hunted for the spot that looked like the one on the diagram. I silently reflected on the many times I'd seen him efficiently change tires for people, in the days when jacks and spare tires were the same for most vehicles.

A pick-up stopped. A thirty-something, broad-shouldered farmer with a kind face got out and walked toward us. "I called my wife on my cell phone and told her I'd be late," he said. "I told her I was stopping to help some people having trouble along the road."

Orv stood up. With the jack in one hand, he reached out to shake hands with the other. The young man took the jack and lay down beside the car. Efficiently he put it in place without the help of diagrams. Relieved and embarrassed, we stood by the road and watched him.

"Be careful," he cautioned. "Don't get hit by a car."

In moments he removed the flat. The metal mesh of the radial tire had come through in many places.

"Be careful with this," he said. "It could really cut your hands."

Orv put the spare in place and the young man put the flat in the back of the van. He showed me the mesh again, and told me to remind my husband not to cut his hand. At that moment, I came to terms with what I had been suspecting for some time. I am in the middle of one of life's many transitions. The man did not stop to help me because I am a woman. He stopped because we looked like two rather helpless senior citizens.

I wanted to tell him that we had delivered a china closet earlier in the day; one that my husband had refinished and that together we had rebuilt the back, the bottom and the legs. I wanted to say that in spite of my unsteadiness the two of us had carried it into someone's basement and eventually we would have figured out how to change that tire. I wanted to tell him we know enough not to be hit by a car, and that we both know what steel-belted radials are. But his face was so full of decency and concern that I knew any indignation was not directed toward him, but toward ourselves.

We thanked him graciously and offered payment for his trouble. He did not accept anything, just as Orv had never accepted payment for the many times he had helped others.

I asked for his name and address, so I could send him a note expressing our deep gratitude. I wanted him to know we were not past the age of good manners. As soon as he left, I quickly scribbled his name on a piece of paper so I wouldn't forget. Unfortunately I lost the paper and did forget who he was after all.

The next time we get a vehicle I think we'll study the instruction book. If we can possibly remember what it says, we'll be better prepared for trouble. I hate looking like two old people who don't know how to change a tire.

Restocking the Taylor Shop

Orv and I planned a three-day buying trip to replenish the shelves in our antique shop. We visited Okoboji, Estherville, West Des Moines, Boonesville, Denison, Walnut, Orange City, and Rock Valley.

Before we set out, Orv counted the pieces of furniture that he needed to refinish. There were thirty-one. We decided to leave the trailer home so we wouldn't be tempted to buy large pieces. We needed only small items so the Dodge hatchback would be ample to hold our purchases. However, we were unable to resist an oak commode in Boonesville and a small walnut desk in Walnut, so we packed crocks, bowls, pictures, churns, art pottery, and three coffee mills in and around them.

At last one shop seemed to merge with the other shops and one dealer with another, until it seemed impossible to tell what was purchased where. Finally with energy and bank account spent, we were eager to get our treasures home.

I leaned back in my seat and allowed the motion of the car to lull me into a fitful sleep. In my dreams I journeyed once more through malls, shops, flea markets, and one whole town where stores almost exclusively stocked antiques.

In my dream-filled state, our identities began to merge with the other shopkeepers and our shop with places we had visited. Then suddenly a bump in the road startled me to wakefulness. Still confused about where we were and who we might be, I cast a fleeting glance at Orv to see if he had grown a mustache, a potbelly, or curly hair. Seeing him sitting calmly at the wheel brought his essence into focus. Momentarily I wondered if my own hair was blond, long, or totally gray, all the while conjecturing whether I was the easy dealer who gave large discounts or the tough dealer who gave none. I checked the mirror to see just how I really looked and then combed my hair so my husband would not guess at my confusion.

At home we unpacked, cleaned, priced, and recorded purchases for hours. Our labor was enhanced with comments such as:

"Oh, I remember the guy who sold us these bean pots. He was set up in that converted schoolhouse in the country."

"Weren't those great shops in West Des Moines? A bit too pricey for us to buy for resale, but certainly worth seeing."

"I loved the bed and breakfast, such interesting conversations and good food."

With items priced and placed on our floors and shelves, I knew who we were again, and I had clear images of the places we had visited. I also knew that, depending on the item or my mood, I am at times the easy dealer and at other times the tough one.

Dream Vacation, 2001

For more than a year, we'd made vacation plans. On September 12, 2001, we would embark on a dream vacation to the eastern seaboard of Newfoundland. We pored over maps, read study guides, and sought information on the Internet. We planned to go whale watching and to see the fjords, the lighthouses, and the bird sanctuaries. We looked forward to traveling east to the assumed landing spot of Leif Erickson and his Viking seamen.

I'd taught social studies for about twenty years. Along with my fifth graders, I learned much about the United States, Canada and Latin America through textbooks and research. Our family often toured the western states in the summer months, but seldom ventured east of the Mississippi. I looked forward to retirement years when we would be able to travel to New England and eastern Canada in the fall. I wanted to see historic places, the Appalachian Mountains in the United States and the Laurentian Highlands in Canada. Through our travels, I could bring textbook information to life in glorious autumn colors. So during retirement years, my husband and I often traveled east, each time seeking out places that we had never seen.

Once we became acquainted with the manager of a small motel and restaurant in New Brunswick. He was a retired officer of the Royal Canadian Mounted Police with many stories to tell, including information about Newfoundland. He filled us in on places we would love to see and encouraged us to go there. We were headed for Prince Edward Island that summer to visit *Anne of Green Gables* country and didn't have the time to add Newfoundland to that outing. However, his urging and his stories intrigued us so much that we soon began to make plans to go there.

On the morning of September 11, 2001, I had not listened to the news before I drove downtown to pick up a few things at the hardware store. The car radio shocked me with the reality that suicide planes had hit the Twin Towers and the Pentagon. The first ones I discussed the national tragedy with that day were the men at the store. By the time I arrived home, Orv also was aware of the tragedy on our own shores. We spent the rest of the day watching telecasts, visiting with family and friends, and packing the car. All the while, we could not quite decide if it would be wise to set out on such a long trip at a time of national crisis. But with a year of planning invested in the trip plus reservations at several places, we hesitated to give all of that up.

Starting cautiously the next morning, we wondered what the mood of the country and the gas prices might be. Each day we edged east, and each evening we made decisions about the following day. When President Bush first addressed the nation, we were in an antique mall in Clarence, New York. With a small group of strangers, we gathered mutely around a small black and white television set. Connected in our collective grief, shock, and confusion, we listened speechlessly.

Crossing the Canadian border was a bit of a decision, but we ventured on. There we were moved to see American and Canadian flags flying together, everywhere. We visited St. John's and Gander, Newfoundland on separate days. American planes had been re-routed to both cities after the New York airports were closed on September 11. Later television documentaries verified what the Canadians had recounted to us a week or so after the event. Upon landing, passengers were obliged to stay on board until all planes were down. By the time the travelers disembarked, the Newfoundlanders in both Gander and St. John's had laid out sumptuous buffets of food for the passengers as they exited the planes and entered the terminals.

Because their waters have been over-fished and present attitudes about furs, the economy of Newfoundland has suffered greatly. Those two important industries once made the province thrive. In spite of that, the citizens opened their hearts and homes to people who could not find lodging in crowded hotels, motels and inns.

As was our usual habit while traveling, we visited antique shops and filled the van with resale items, purchased on both sides of the border. My most prized purchase on that trip was a piece I bought for myself in St. John's, a nine-inch soapstone statue of an Inuit and whale. We were accustomed from previous trips to keeping receipts to present at the border. We had heard of difficult experiences with border investigations from other travelers, but fortunately we never had one bit of trouble with the crossing.

We did see the bird sanctuaries, the puffins, and the fjords. We became more acquainted with Newfoundland's history in museums and other places of interest. We gathered information about exploration and early settlement along with facts about First Nation People. We talked to hardy fellows stacking timber along roadsides and to local patrons in small restaurants. We bought books about the various provinces and visited a living history Viking Village, located on the spot Leif Erickson and his crew are said to have landed around the year 1000. They taught us a few Viking games and showed us how to cook over an open fire in order to make a type of pancake, things typical of the Viking era. But the whales eluded us, spouting from distances too far out for our boats to venture. It was October and their migration had begun.

The ferry rides, the lighthouses, and the people were all that we had hoped for and more. We traveled over 6500 miles in our Dodge minivan and rode three ferries for a total of more than twenty-four hours. We met interesting people in restaurants and dinner theaters. The trip was indeed a dream vacation, but we were constantly aware of the nightmare in the lives of many. America had been attacked on our own shores, and the world was forever changed.

The World According to Garth

We met Garth in 1994. Orv and I were newly retired, he from sales and I from teaching school. We were working at establishing an antique shop as a retirement business to give us something productive to do. Off on a long-awaited fall trip to New England, we intended to tour historic Boston and watch the leaves turn color in the Allegheny Mountains and the Berkshire Hills. To enhance the trip we would seek out items to buy for our shop.

In an antique mall, somewhere in Pennsylvania, a shopkeeper whose face and name I no longer recall, advised us to go to Clarence, New York, just East of Buffalo. He told us Clarence is full of antique shops and every Sunday, year round, they hold a flea market. If the weather is good, hundreds of vendors unload trucks, pick-ups, vans, and car trunks, to sell goods under trees and in the open air.

The weekend was approaching, so we decided to re-route through Clarence. We didn't know the area, arrived after dark on a Saturday, and stumbled onto a nondescript motel where I slept uncomfortably and fitfully. I awakened early, fully ready to get out of that room and go before dawn. I speculated that perhaps there were more fleas in our room than at the market. We arrived at the poorly lit grounds in the dark and adjusted our vision to the six or eight buildings and a roofed walkway, which offered permanent space for certain dealers. Vendors were scattered about the grounds selling home-canned jams and jellies, flowers, T-shirts, new and used tools, Hummel figurine look-alikes made in China, antiques, collectibles, and cholesterol-laden lunches.

One vendor with a firm voice kept announcing, "Everything is half price or less."

We studied her inventory and bought a custard glass spooner, a pink depression-glass cracker jar, and a teapot. At other spots we purchased some homemade gooseberry jam, silhouettes, a three-gallon Western crock, and collectible prints.

In one of the buildings we ran into a dealer we know from Sioux Falls, South Dakota. He was there with a large truck, and he was buying furniture from Garth. We were there with a Dodge Caravan with no back seats, but soon we too were buying furniture from Garth. He sold us a blanket chest, a hall seat with a mirror and coat hooks, and a parlor table with ball-and-claw feet. Orv took the table apart to save space. Then he loaded the drawers of the chest and the bench of the hall seat with our smaller treasures. We traded pleasantries and also traded a tobacco grinder, which we had bought in Arkansas earlier that year, and several pieces of pottery that did not sell well in Iowa. Then we headed for Boston.

The leaves and the Appalachian Mountains were all we hoped for, so the next fall we traveled east again. We wanted to cross the St. Lawrence River and vacation in Ontario and Quebec, but we carefully planned our route to go through Clarence on a Sunday. We bought lamps, vases, flatirons, iron banks, a cast iron Dutch oven, and more teapots. The woman with all items half-price or less was there again, hoping to lessen her inventory before it rained. I bought a couple of finger lamps and a stoneware toothbrush holder from her. Then we looked for Garth.

He remembered us, and the tobacco grinder. Orv asked him if it sold well.

"I took it to an auction," he said. "No one wanted to buy it here."

"Did you make any money on it?"

"I don't know," said Garth. "I don't check individual items. I just check the bottom line."

He told us business was rotten. That no one wants to pay what his things are worth and when he buys merchandise the sellers all have high opinions of their own things. He wore his bad luck like a badge of honor behind a bit of a grin, and I could never quite tell when he was kidding or when he was serious. Still, when it came to the bottom line, Garth always treated us well. We bought another hall seat and some portraits of grim-looking people, because we wanted the large oak and gesso picture frames around them.

In the following years we continued to vacation in the East every fall. We checked out Bar Harbor, Kennebunkport, Nova Scotia, Prince Edward Island, and Newfoundland. We took lighthouse tours, went to museums and bird sanctuaries, listened to lectures, attended dinner theaters, and picked up smooth stones at different spots on each of the Great Lakes. We checked out hundreds of antiques shops, visited the House of Seven Gables, and the home of Anne of Green Gables. We rode excursion boats and ferries, and went whale watching. We ate up countless miles in four different Dodge Caravans through the years. Each time we left the back seats at home, and each time we went east, we planned a stop at Clarence on a weekend.

Most of the vendors at the flea market seemed unremarkable and I couldn't remember if I had seen them the previous year or not. But there was always the woman with everything for half price or less and there was always Garth. He sold us six or eight hall seats through the years as well as cupboards, mirrors, tables, sideboards and every now and then portraits of grim-looking people in outstanding frames. As he got to know us better he talked more and more about the *system* and the unfairness of life.

In 2001, we arrived in Clarence in mid-September. All of America was shaken. On the Saturday after 9-11, we watched President Bush address the nation on a small black and white TV in The Clarence Courtyard Antique Mall. A dozen or more customers stood mutely in front of that TV set, each thinking private thoughts. I thought about my grandchildren and wondered if I should have stayed home. The next day we talked to Garth. He wanted to bomb someone, but he wasn't sure whom.

He said, "The country is lucky that I'm not president, because I'm so mad that I'd be sure to make some bad decisions."

I'll never forget that conversation, but I don't remember detailed purchases from 2001. Still, as in other years, I know we did not leave Garth's space empty-handed.

In 2003, he sold us two Red Riding Hood cookie jars and a couple of china cabinets, one with a broken glass. We loaded the cookie jars, but we had already bought too many other pieces to get the cabinets into the van. We tried in vain to rent a U-Haul. Five different places in Buffalo said they had none available. Garth offered to give our money back, or keep the cabinets until later with no charge for storage. We thought it over while we combed the flea market for more small items; then we went back to Garth's space and told him we had decided to leave them and come back another time.

As the months went on, we called him several times to let him know we would not leave them indefinitely. He gave us his usual litany of bad luck, and told us how hard it is to get good merchandise, and how the system is completely wrong.

Once when Orv asked him about profits, he said, "There were lots of prophets, Elijah, Mohammed, and plenty of false prophets. The ones I talk to are prophets of gloom and doom. I've got to quit hanging around with those guys, they're affecting my attitude."

In May we called to tell him we were getting ready to sell at an antique show, but we would come in June to pick up the cabinets. We urged him to try to find another hall seat for us. He said they were hard to find and too expensive. Then he added, "I just had a vision. You are going to sell well at the antique show."

Early in June we finally made it back to Clarence. The woman with everything for half price or less had upgraded to a space in the roofed-in walkway. She had also upgraded to three categories: a five-dollar table, a ten-dollar table, and a table with everything half price or less. She sold me two pictures, a green Depression glass reamer, a porcelain cracker jar, and a milk pitcher that looks like a cow. My bill came to seventy-one dollars so she took off another dollar and charged just seventy.

Garth's building was full, but he had our china cabinets pushed aside in a corner. After we greeted each other he showed us where they were. "You remember the one with the broken glass?" he asked. I nodded and he went on to say, "Well it's still broke."

He had found another hall seat for us. We exchanged pleasantries and then tried to exchange a pair of Victorian chairs we had not been able to sell in Iowa. We had noticed their type often in the East and hoped to find a market for them. However, two other shopkeepers had already refused them.

Orv sized up our space and decided if he dismantled some of the furniture, we could also buy a buffet and a five-legged table. Garth shot us a price and we offered him fifty dollars less and suggested that he take our chairs. Garth was not interested. His price was fair so we made the deal his way, thinking we would either peddle the chairs elsewhere or donate them to The Salvation Army.

Orv has his own way of loading and he doesn't like to talk while working. I advised Garth that we should leave him alone. While we waited I looked at a small Victorian parlor table with a marble top. I usually buy one piece for myself on a trip and I liked that table. Garth told me they used to sell for three hundred dollars but now people don't want "good stuff." They want things with paint falling off and '50s tables with chrome legs. He offered it to me for two hundred. I was pleased with the price, but hesitated, wondering if we would have room. While I was thinking, Garth came down another twenty-five dollars. I checked with Orv, about space. He thought he could work it in, and the deal was done.

When I handed Garth the check, he said, "If you want to leave the chairs I'll sell them for you and send you the money."

Orv replied, "That's the best offer we've had," and went back to his packing.

Garth and I wandered back into the building where he told me about his fifteen-year-old son, a gifted draftsman with a lot of talent, who had quit school. Garth told me that he had dropped out of school himself, but wanted better for his boy. He told me about moving into a new home and described in detail some of the unusual pieces of furniture they owned. I told him about our family, our shop at home and booths in an antique mall, my husband's careers in farming and sales and mine as a mother, grandmother and teacher.

Eventually the conversation went to private business and then to co-ops. Garth informed me that he hated all co-ops, especially co-op antique malls, which were run by a bunch of communists and schoolteachers. I laughed and checked out his expression. It never changed.

Then to my surprise Garth quietly pulled his bankroll out of his front pocket and handed me a fifty-dollar bill. "Will this do for the chairs?" he asked.

After the car was packed we once more worked our way through the vendors for a few small items. Garth told us to leave our purchases with him until we were through shopping. He had us put them in a safe place because "There are lots of jerks around here with a capital J."

When we left the flea market Garth was sitting on his chair, feet up, waiting for customers who would not pay him what his things were worth.

"Did you have a good day?" Orv asked him.

"You've heard of karma?" Garth asked. "Well I got bad karma. In fact right now it's so bad that whatever is coming will be better than this."

I didn't realize it at the time, but that was to be our last long trip east. Health issues soon kept me from enjoying the rides. Yet, at times I entertain pensive thoughts about traveling through New England and eastern Canada, and routing our trip through Clarence on a weekend. Maybe we could still buy a few items for half price or less, some outstanding picture frames with grim-looking portraits, and make a few deals with Garth.

Collections

Once I collected rocks
and paper dolls
the kind that
talked to me.

Later I amassed
bells, books, prints
tea pots, Victorian furniture
paper weights
and several extra pounds.

I still like rocks, especially
amethysts, tourmalines
and diamonds.

Among my prints
are three paper dolls
complete with paper wardrobes.

Now I try to balance
one thing against another
not having room for all
then re-collect my senses—
letting go.

Morning Glory

Just past dawn,
collecting thoughts and vigor
I hike familiar paths
amid grasses, reeds
and Queen Anne's Lace.

Touched by night rain
and morning dew—
an array of spider webs
gives grandeur
to the landscape.

Yesterday, unseen and drab
today be-jeweled and brilliant
yet rendered briefly useless
for catching spider meals.

Their garnered glory
unseen in useful times.

A Time
to Grow

Shades of Tom Sawyer

No one ever told me to whitewash a fence. No one even suggested that I paint one. When I did become engaged in that project, it did not occur to me to manipulate anyone into helping me paint it. But the old iron fence on the west and south sides of our lawn intrigued me, and I often thought of ways to make it look better.

The posts were hollow iron rods, topped by pointed finials. Supporting rods joined the posts just below those finials. A six-inch decorative sleeve was in the center of each supporting rod. The fence itself was made of twisted iron, thin enough to be woven into a pattern with arches between the posts. It had likely been installed when the farmhouse was built in the mid-1890s near our small northwest Iowa town. The fence remained untouched for more than fifty years, so by 1950, though still attractive, it was rusty.

It occurred to me that I could paint the posts and connecting rods black. Then I would paint parts of the finials, the decorative sleeve, and the woven fence with aluminum paint.

My parents had come through the hard times of the Great Depression and two World Wars. They had weathered illnesses and losses, which caused them to remain forever conscious of the importance of spending carefully and wisely, so I was accustomed to being nixed on projects that might cost money.

Still, my father was aware that keeping the farm buildings in good condition was a good investment in the long run, and they had all recently received fresh coats of paint. I could imagine that the whole effect would be improved if I would paint that fence.

By that time I was a high school sophomore and hard times were over, the farm was paid for, and a few luxuries began to appear. A Monarch gas range had replaced the old wood and coal cook stove in the kitchen. We had electricity, a refrigerator and for the first time in his life, Dad bought a new car—a blue '49 Ford with lots of chrome, a push button radio and overdrive. I decided it was safe to approach him on the idea of buying paint for the fence.

"Paint the fence?" It had never occurred to Dad or anyone else.

"If you buy the paint, I'll do the whole thing myself. I can even get credit for the job in my 4-H record book."

Small cash awards were given at the Osceola County Fair for record books that showed some initiative. That would be an added plus, but it was not my main motivation. I could really envision how nice that old fence would look.

I was known as the family fidget, impatient with tedious projects. My mother used to say my piano practice sessions ended in thunderstorms before I stomped out of the house and looked for some tree to climb. Mercifully she allowed me to give up on those lessons by the time I was eleven.

I was likely to throw sewing projects in the corner when things didn't go together smoothly. Often I would return later and finish the projects after I had cooled down, but at times, my mother or sister would finish for me. Dad had good reasons to wonder if I had enough patience to finish the job once I started.

I might have caught him on a good day, or maybe he could see that I was growing up, and perhaps he, too, was tired of not spending a few dollars on things that would give no return for his investment. Whatever his motivation, he decided to indulge me and bought the paint, a little at a time, just in case I decided to quit before the job was done.

I had to dig out and pull grass growing in the fence line, then clear soil from around the bottom parts of the woven iron wires. I did a few sections at a time, clearing, digging, and painting. It was intriguing to see my masterpiece develop and a lot more rewarding than playing the piano or sewing feed sack dresses. To Dad's surprise and good pleasure, I stuck with the job day after day, except when it rained.

I cleaned all parts of the fence with a wire brush, and then gave the woven parts a wide sweep with the silvery colored paint as my paintbrush bounced from one wire to another. Then I'd climb the fence and repeat the process on the other side. There was no way for me to avoid the spatters bouncing from my brush. Certain areas, like the arches, demanded more careful attention. Applying the black paint to the uprights and connecting rods was tedious, as I needed to avoid getting black paint on other parts of the fence.

As one section and then another began to take shape, other family members started to show some interest. By the time I was a little more than half finished with the south section of the fence, it no longer seemed like one of "Betty's crazy ideas." My sister Esther was home from college that summer. She was likely to be sewing clothes, playing the piano, or helping with summer canning, but from time to time she joined me in the project. She was more patient than I, and ended the day with fewer spatters on her face, arms and clothing.

My brother, Gordon, was married earlier that summer, so I had a new sister-in-law. Marge enjoyed getting in on things. Before long she had a brush in her hand. My mother, whose health was never robust, couldn't get down on the ground to paint. Still she showed up at times, took hold of a brush and painted connecting rods and the tops of the posts. Dad and Gordon were otherwise occupied with farm work, but sometimes wandered over to admire the fence and offer words of encouragement.

"You're doing a good job. It's really shaping up."

"I'm proud of you for sticking to it."

"You have black paint on your nose."

Neighbors, friends, and extended family members commented on the improvements about the place.

Unlike Tom Sawyer, I did do the lion's share of the job, but family members had made the job less tedious. We had a shared pride when the fence was finally finished. My parents never ceased to extol the virtues of scrimping, saving, not wasting, and making do, but they never regretted spending a few frivolous dollars on what Dad often referred to as "Betty's fence."

Reorientation

For six years in a one-room school
my orientation always was the same.
Maps and blackboards to the north
cloak room to the south
green fields to the east
and my home through the westward window.

Oiled floors squeaked beneath my feet.
Desks bolted to it
stained with spilled Scripto
were grooved and initialed
from years of careless use.

A globe suspended from the ceiling
counter-balanced by an iron weight
offered a limited global view
for a child who daydreamed
through science, history, and geography.

Washington and Lincoln looked down at me
with unseeing eyes focused
more on a vision of America
than the discomfiture of elementary students.
Just below them was the alphabet
in perfect Palmer method
that I could never duplicate.

At the recitation bench I mastered
arithmetic, spelling
and how to read with expression.
A scratchy wind-up phonograph
led us in "Frog Went A Courtin'"
and "Camptown Races."
On the playground I dealt with relationships
learned that life's not always fair
and how to give and take.

We took our turns at carrying water in a bucket
for the Red Wing cooler
or coal in a scuttle for the heater
that stood in the middle of the room.
We dusted erasers and washed blackboards
and valued those responsibilities.

Since then I've visited two oceans
the Mississippi and the Great Salt Lake.
I observed Greenland from a jet, stood
at the summit of Pikes Peak
took a launch through the Everglades and
looked upward at the General Sherman Tree.
I experienced the enchantment of London
Quebec City and Acapulco.
I've learned to fear for rain forests in Brazil
global warming, acid rain, and nuclear reactors.

When my not-so-limited global view disturbs
my dreams both day and night
when I long for simpler times and
a more distinct orientation
when my directions never were confused
I close my eyes and seem to draw the vision
Maps and blackboards to the north
cloakroom to the south
farm fields to the east
and my home through the westward window.

The Land Between Two Rivers

Where once was found a wild and free domain
tall grass prairies stretched, untamed and wide
intruders came in wagons, or on trains
plowed earth and built a heritage of pride.
They constructed roads, rails, and handsome homes
developed farmland, churches, schools, and towns
where the Sioux, the elk, and bison freely roamed
and wildlife in profusion did abound.

Through years of struggle they would realize
dreams of a fine, desired place to be.
The countryside became quite civilized
a place to educate and raise a family.

But pasque flowers in the spring might raise their heads
and wonder why the prairie grass is dead.

"Owed" to Snow

In my early years I couldn't wait to see
the season when alluring snow would fall.
It meant fox and geese games to my friends and me
or the joy of packing snow into a ball.
Then as cold arctic winds consumed the day
when the old house could not dispel the cold
I found less joy in going out to play
benumbing days were cheerless, dark and old.

Yet even now as I watch seasons pass
and know that winter has a side that's down
I seldom dwell on how long it may last
as I watch first flakes blanketing the ground.

Though passing years have urged gray hair to grow
I dream of making angels in the snow.

Next Best Thing to a Pony

One of the boys in our neighborhood rode a Shetland pony to school. We kids were envious, but knew better than to ask for one for ourselves. There never seemed to be extra money for things we didn't really need. Imagine our surprise when the next best thing to a pony came into our lives—and more than one at that. Two of Dad's workhorses produced foals.

We girls had not been informed that births would be forthcoming, and it was certainly not considered an important part of our education to watch the birthing process. We were simply informed that the foals were there, we could go to the barn to see them but were not to disturb the mares.

Mary was a pretty sorrel, somewhat smaller than the other horses. She gave birth to an equally pretty sorrel filly with a white spot on her forehead. The foal seemed to be an almost royal creature so we named her Duchess. She grew to hold her head proudly and developed a gait fitting with her name.

Bess, a strawberry roan, produced a blue roan colt. It seemed logical that Dad would eventually use them as a team so we thought the names should go together. We called him Duke.

Gordon, Esther, and I, the three youngest of the family, played with the foals incessantly, both in their stalls and around the yard. Somewhere along the line, I learned that Duke had become a gelding, but I didn't know what that meant or how it came about. By the time they were big enough to support our weight, they were so tame that we had no trouble mounting them. Dad supervised us at first, but eventually trusted us to be careful and not to get hurt while riding. His trust was not always justified, but we survived and so did the horses.

Because they were so tame, it was easy for Dad to break them to harness and convince them to pull when they were big and strong enough. By that time, riding bareback was a challenge as my legs weren't long enough to grip the horse's sides and stay on easily. Still, one Sunday afternoon when we were looking for some amusement, we asked for permission to ride the horses about the farm.

Due to the mild temperaments of Duke and Duchess, our parents agreed. Gordon helped us girls mount the filly. Esther was in front holding on to the reins, and I was behind her holding on to Esther.

Gordon mounted Duke, and we rode out to the fields at a leisurely pace. Everything went well, with no hi-jinx for a change. There I was atop what had been a foal, but now a full-grown horse with quite a girth. With my legs sticking out on both sides, there was nothing to grip but my sister.

As my tenuous hold on the horse loosened, my grip on Esther tightened, and soon both of us were on the ground with a large workhorse above us. Duchess' hind foot missed me, but stepped on Esther's long hair, barely missing her head. Hearing our cries, Gordon sized up the situation, dismounted, and sent the horses home. The three of us, unharmed but shaken, walked slowly back to the farmyard.

Our equally shaken parents, who had seen horses come back with no riders, met us with the car as we trudged home. The horror of what might have happened left us all a bit mute as Mom washed the dirt from Esther's hair. Everything was pretty quiet for the rest of the day, and several days after.

Queen and Mary produced foals again another summer. Mom and Dad thought we might play with them as we had the others, but we were older and had gone on to other things. I don't even recall what we named them or what their markings might have been.

Dad had a bit more trouble breaking them when they were ready to pull, but as in other areas of farming, he was equal to the challenge. It seemed we were just as well off without a pony, as our love affair with horses had long since faded.

Images, Stained in Glass

Before a white altar
in a white frame church
in a long white robe
symbolic of the Holy Spirit
dwelling in me
at age thirteen
I first received the Eucharist.

From a stained glass window
above the altar
Christ Himself welcomed me
with outstretched arms.
From time to time I am beckoned
back to the white frame church
for weddings, anniversaries
and four solemn trips
up and down its aisle
behind the caskets of my closest kin.

In its pews I am the eternal child
allowing my eyes and mind
to wander from the sermon
searching the stained glass
Christ above the altar.
I study as I did in childhood
the panes that don't quite match
since being replaced
after a hailstorm in the forties.

Like those panes I have a sense
of not quite belonging
as if too much of me has been replaced
and the image of myself is not so clearly defined
as that of the thirteen-year-old confirmand.

Then I hear my father's voice
sweetened now from years of singing
with the heavenly chorus
intoning his favorite hymn
"Just as I am Without One Plea."

Just as I am Lord
with broken parts replaced
not quite matching
yet more precious to you
than stained glass counterpanes
hold me in Your gracious hands.

Landmark Recollections

As a student at Augustana College in Sioux Falls, South Dakota, I had an intermittent association with the Cataract Hotel. During the years of 1952 to 1954, several of my friends and I waited tables for special occasions in its stately banquet room.

When I mention the Cataract Hotel these days, I often get strange looks and disbelieving chuckles. Most people associate cataracts with eye surgery, forgetting that a waterfall is also a cataract. The hotel and the city were both named for an enchanting falls, which tumbles over red quartzite rocks in the Sioux River.

The original Cataract Hotel on Ninth Street and Phillips Avenue was built in 1871. It was small by today's standards with fourteen rooms, but it carried a reputation of being the finest hotel in the area. Second and third Cataract Hotels were built on that site, perhaps all three standing at one time. In 1899, following a destructive fire, plans were made for an elegant stone building, as well as an improved fire department for the city. The fourth and last Cataract was finished in 1901. It stood proudly in downtown Sioux Falls until urban renewal dictated its demise in the early seventies.

House numbers that do not coincide with street numbers often confuse visitors to Sioux Falls. The numbering system came about in 1886 when the Cataract was considered the center of the town, prompting house numeration to start at the intersection of Ninth Street and Phillips Avenue. The confusing system is still in use.*

As waitresses in the banquet room, we had rules to follow. We were required to wear white blouses with black skirts, nylon stockings, and black shoes. Nylons of the day had seams going up the backs of the legs and were held in place with garter belts.

The dining room hostess was in charge of our duties. She was as elegant as the room itself and spoke with a British accent. Her hair had one streak of silver disappearing into a wave of black. Meticulously, she taught us to use a bit of grace, stressing that we should stand behind the diner to serve from the right and remove from the left. And once after a wedding, she let us taste the champagne punch.

As we moved from the banquet room into the kitchen things became more basic. The chef surprised me. He was not tall and handsome like the French chefs in the movies, but short and dumpy with a soiled apron. I knew he must be the chef because the hat was right. He spoke with a grumpy accent, and I never once saw him kiss his fingers after tasting the soup.

As far back in the kitchen as possible was a woman who scraped plates and operated the dishwasher. Her hair was stuffed under a net and a ragged apron covered her rounded abdomen. Her shoes looked like they had come from Salvation Army's bargain basement, and her cotton stockings were rolled on elastic garters, which held them up, just below her knees.

I thought she looked to be about my mother's age, and wondered what kind of unkempt piece of space she might call home—or if anyone had ever loved her. The half-used cigarettes and elegant foods seemed irresistible. She might pick up a previously used spoon to eat the remnants of decorated cakes and portions of ice cream shaped like flowers or fruit, or enjoy a few puffs left in the cigarettes. We awkwardly avoided eye contact as she savored sumptuous foods not ordinarily a part of her diet.

When the weather permitted, we walked the twenty-eight blocks downtown from Augustana and back again to save a twenty-five cent bus fare. On one of those return trips, after waiting tables for several hours, my friend Patty and I, in a tired fit of silliness, stepped out of the group and our shoes. We released our garters, took off our nylons in public, and walked back to the dorm with bare feet. Our friends went to the other side of the street and pretended not to know us. They forgave us by the next time we were called to work, as they needed our help.

Today the Wells Fargo Building, a rather cold-looking structure with lots of glass in the façade, stands in the place of the old hotel. It serves quite a different purpose and is certainly not the hub of the city. Had the Cataract survived a few more years, preservationists might have saved it as they did the old Shriver-Johnson's Department Store and many other historic buildings.

I liked going downtown to the Sioux Falls of the fifties. It offered convenient bus service, dress shops, movie theater, Carnegie Library, Woolworths, Fantles, and department stores with mezzanines.

I'm not comfortable driving among all the cars on Forty-first Street, and I find the busy-ness of the Empire Mall quite disconcerting. My grandchildren who live there love Sioux Falls as it is now. They once explored the bike paths, played sports at the YMCA, attended large high schools, and feel comfortable in the mall and other large shopping areas. They don't have lunch on a mezzanine, but enjoy food courts, Wendy's, IHOP, Minerva's, and HuHot. Their stories about Sioux Falls will be quite different from mine when they talk to their grandchildren. They will never know what great times they missed.

*www. Greetings from the Cataract Hotel
www.siouxfalls.org/Information/history/trivia/triva_questions
www.augie.edu/CWS/sesqui.html

High Pockets
Legendary Character in Sioux Falls

I used to see her in downtown Sioux Falls.
Her alone-ness made her an oddity
to college kids
who mostly functioned in groups.

She was a large, raw-boned woman
with ample feet encased
in men's high-topped boots.
She wore a tattered, slightly feminine hat
but her most notable attire
was a well-worn coat
with large and roomy pockets.

Once when my friends and I
were admiring wedding dresses
in Shriver-Johnson's window
High Pockets walked by.

She observed us as she approached
and then dismissed us with a comment
"Cheap veneer," she taunted
and laughed halfway down the block.

Circle of Friends

From 1954 to 1956, I was a two-year elementary education student at Augustana College in Sioux Falls, South Dakota. During that time I made friends with other young women who were enrolled in the same program.

We were full of life, untried opinions, optimism, and faith. We had no idea that we would travel unexpected paths or come to terms with situations more shocking and profound than we could imagine.

Insecurities replaced any feelings of privilege we might have entertained about going to college. Most of my new circle of friends came from small towns within a hundred-mile radius of Sioux Falls. Towns with names like Inwood, Westbrook, Lake Wilson, Eagan, and Irene.

While four-year students studied liberal arts during their first two years, we were thrust into classes with other two-year students, preparing for more immediate job opportunities. Besides mandatory Christianity classes, we carried heavy course loads, including one semester with Saturday morning classes. Because we were together in almost every class, we learned to know each other well.

We gathered in groups around a coffee pot on someone's hot plate each evening for devotions and bonding. Patty, Janice, LaVonne, Verna, Mary, Audrey, Margaret and I formed lasting friendships that have continued throughout our lives.

Because we expected to be there for only two years, we were not invited to join certain organizations or to try out for the best choir on campus. Those groups were interested in forming bases of students who would be enrolled for a longer period of time. We took jobs at the library and the cafeteria, cleaned offices and homes, baby-sat, and waited tables.

Our lives were full of subtle dichotomies. The United States was not officially at war, but it was engaged in a Police Action in Korea where people were killed in huge numbers, just as if there had been a real war. Ballroom dancing and square dancing were not allowed on campus. Still, we were allowed square games with promenades and do-si-dos exactly the same as those in square dances. The college frowned on sororities or fraternities. Yet they sponsored rush week followed by invitations to join societies with Greek initials exactly like those in fraternities and sororities. Women were not allowed to smoke in the dorms, but men were.

The Dean of Women informed us that Augustana girls should not be seen in blue jeans, so in spite of cold walks we always wore skirts to classes. All of us owned blue jeans and sweatshirts, but wore them only in the dorms or perhaps to the library. If we felt rebellious we would put on our jeans and Augustana sweatshirts, to ride a city bus or to walk the twenty-eight blocks downtown, feeling deliciously wicked.

Margaret Benson was my sophomore roommate. She was always pleasant, but I seemed to sense sadness behind the smiles. Because of the mild segregation we experienced, I was not likely to venture deeply into campus life, but she made the best of it. To be more actively involved, she joined "B" choir and one of the less prestigious societies with Greek letters.

We chose nicknames for each other, often shortened down to last names or one syllable, thus Margaret became Mugs. Together, we could laugh at everything and nothing. Yet our conservative backgrounds somewhat defined us, and daily trips to chapel and nightly devotions in our dorm rooms strengthened us. We shared our past and our dreams for the future.

Mugs told us that her mother was confined to a wheel chair, and her father was a postal worker who had heart problems. Her older sister had a four-year degree and their parents wanted four years of college for Mugs. They said they would manage it somehow, but because of their health issues, she opted for a two-year course.

During that time, her father was frequently hospitalized several blocks from campus in the Veterans Hospital. Mugs and LaVonne often took the city bus or walked to see him. A few hours after one such visit, Margaret was summoned to the telephone at the end of our third floor in Tuve Hall. Without a word, she grabbed some Kleenex and headed for the phone. As she feared, a nurse from the VA was calling to tell her that her father was gone. At age nineteen, Margaret shouldered the responsibility of calling her mother and sister to inform them of his death. She went home to help with funeral arrangements. Within ten days she was back in school.

The sad look in Mugs' eyes seemed even more noticeable, but she still had her sense of humor and spirit. She brought her father's car so she could go home on weekends, but one weekend she and LaVonne took the car to visit LaVonnne's home in a small Minnesota town called Lake Wilson. Clad in their jeans, and smoking, they were off for a much-needed, lighthearted time. At one point Mugs flipped a cigarette through the open window, unaware that the butt flipped right back in. Suddenly the friends smelled smoke and noticed a fire in the back seat. They were adjacent to one of Minnesota's many lakes, so they drove to it, took out the seat and extinguished the fire.

We looked forward to Graduation Day, but when it came we met the world with as many insecurities as we'd had the day we enrolled as freshmen. My closest friends in the two-year elementary graduating class had secured teaching positions, venturing on to new places. Mugs, however, was going back to her home area. She accepted a teaching position in Lake Andes, South Dakota, near her hometown of Ravinia, in order to take care of her mother. Eight of us started a round robin letter, which we have continued to pass from one to the other in rotation since 1954. That circle was broken early in our lives by Mary's death from cancer when we were in our early thirties.

The rest of us went on with our lives, working, marrying, raising children, but always in touch through letters and reunions. Margaret married a local fellow, Jim Bradley, and continued to look after her mother. After her mother's death they moved to Oregon where they raised two daughters, Rhonda and Paula. Mugs always held a job and was of great strength to her family in every way. I would like to say she lived happily ever after, but history had an unfortunate way of repeating itself. When the children were still home Margaret, like her mother, was diagnosed with multiple sclerosis. Like her father, her husband had a bad heart.

They moved back to South Dakota and made their home in Aberdeen where Jim managed a Legion Club. Whenever I saw Mugs, I still saw that optimistic smile and attitude, plus the ability to laugh in the face of difficulty. Still, the sadness in the eyes was always there as she dealt with the cares of life. Gradually she was forced to accept a cane, a walker, and finally a motorized wheel chair. She laboriously typed letters for our round robin and we were never out of touch.

Time passed, our families grew, our children became adults who were on their own, and some of us became grandmothers. Then one of Margaret's round robin letters arrived with sad news. She recounted the events of the evening she saw Jim slump in his chair. She wrote that she had driven her wheel chair to him and found that he was gone. Once more she dealt with funeral arrangements. Then with the assistance of home health care and her younger daughter Paula, she continued to stay in her home for several years longer than seemed possible.

The last time I saw Mugs was in 1998. LaVonne, Janice, and I met in different towns along the way and drove to Aberdeen to see her. At that time she could move only her head and her left arm. Still she continued to type the round robin letters and send them on. She was a symbol of courage and perseverance to all of us in a way that continues to affect my life, my faith, my compassion, and my understanding of others as well as myself.

Again, history repeated itself. Once Mugs had taken care of her own mother. Now her older daughter, Rhonda, would assume the role of caregiver. Rhonda and her family took Margaret to Texas and hired a nurse for her care during the day.

More typing errors appeared in the letters, but we always looked forward to seeing them in the round robin. In May of 2002 I was delighted when her letter included an e-mail address. Three weeks after our email exchanges began, they ended abruptly. Mugs was gone. She had an unexpected turn in her health and died just two days after entering the hospital. Once more, the circle was broken and we grieved not only for her passing, but also for her difficult and courageous life.

Rhonda and Paula, with their families, took Margaret's ashes back to Aberdeen to be interred beside Jim. At the memorial service the daughters told how Mugs' sense of humor was still present during those last difficult days. She kidded the nurses and told her family not to worry about one nurse who seemed short tempered. The long and difficult story of her life seemed to be over.

Then in May of 2005, one of our friends sent me a letter and a clipping. She had noticed a rather obscure article in the *Sioux Falls Argus Leader* about a Texas woman, formerly of Aberdeen, South Dakota, who had been murdered by the nurse hired to take care of her in the daytime.*

Starting with the brief information from the *Argus Leader* I managed to find several newspaper articles on the Internet from *The Monitor,* in McAllen, Texas. According to one article dated May 29, 2005, Margaret Bradley had died at the hands of Jeanine Hannah, the nurse hired to be her caregiver. Ms. Hannah had lost her license to practice in another state, but found her way to Texas, where she somehow managed to become licensed under an assumed name. Later Rhonda discovered that the nurse had forged checks in order to steal money from Margaret's account.

The remains had been cremated, but blood tests taken at the hospital gave shocking evidence. Margaret had been injected with a lethal dose of insulin. She did not need insulin, but had a

B-12 shot every day. The so-called caregiver had replaced one of the B-12 injections with insulin. Further investigation showed that the woman had been implicated in the death of a patient in Oregon, one who needed insulin and did not get it. She was also accused of patient abuses in nursing homes there. Nothing in Oregon had been proven, so families connected with those people were pleased to see justice done when Hannah was tried and sentenced to ninety-nine years for the murder of Margaret Bradley.

Three years after Margaret's death, we all grieved once more. I have kept her long outdated e-mail address on my computer and the last messages she sent. Her final round robin letter traveled three complete rounds. No one had the heart to take it out. Finally, I made a copy for myself and suggested that LaVonne take the original and keep it.

I have heard it said that people we meet alter our lives forever. They affect the way we think and the way we treat people, as well as our understanding of ourselves as physical and spiritual beings.

Margaret had not taught school for many years, yet from a hospital bed and motorized wheelchair, totally unable to provide her own care, she continued to teach many people about perseverance and faith. The surviving members of our group retain some of our youth and much of our humor. I believe we were altered positively by getting to know Margaret and each other. Our faith and values have sustained us through the years, and we look forward with guarded optimism at what is yet to come.

*SIOUX FALLS ARGUS LEADER Wire Report, May 29, 2005
THE MONITOR, McAllen Texas, May 29, 2005
EDINBURG, Texas (AP)- A 55-year-old former home health care worker has been convicted of killing a former South Dakota resident with insulin after stealing from her.

Remembering Joe Green

In the mid-fifties, life in a Midwest rural community was quite structured. The mothers were all at home, the parents were together, learning was important, and the teacher was in charge of the classroom. At age nineteen, I began my first year of teaching. After earning a two-year associate's degree in elementary education, I was determined to teach the curriculum well.

A family with several children decided to camp along a nearby river and send their children to our small school. One of their sons, a young boy by the name of Joe Green, came into my classroom. He wasn't a noisy boy, but disrupted the flow of my classroom by daydreaming through class discussions, losing his papers and not finishing his work. During the short time he attended I recall being quite intent on getting him to change those habits. Looking back on those years, I don't recall ever having much of a conversation with him about what life was like for a son of transient parents.

I have no idea how they managed to eke out a living, but I do recall that after a couple of weeks, they moved on to another location.

Joe Green continues to haunt me at times. He must be in his sixties now, and I wonder how life has treated him, or if he has ever been able to carve out a so-called normal life.

During twenty-eight years of teaching, other transient children came into my classroom. Perhaps I was never more successful at teaching any of them the rudiments of education, but I talked to them and let them know I cared about the individual as well as the subject matter.

One such student was a dark-haired, dark-eyed girl named Dora. She could read and write well, but her math skills were sorely lacking. I asked her to stay after school so we could work on those. She did not mind at all. The other students were not receptive to her, and I suspect things at home may have been uninviting. In addition to working on math, I made a point to ask her questions about where she had lived before and how many schools she had attended.

She told me she couldn't count them all, and my mind went back to Joe Green. I wondered how many he'd attended. I know I never asked.

Dora and I made little progress on her math, but more progress on forming a friendship. Dora was there less than a week, but we became comfortable with each other. Early one morning before children were admitted into the building, Dora bustled into my classroom carrying a garbage bag, and began stuffing it with personal belongings from her desk.

"I'm leaving," she announced. "The sheriff came and told my dad to get out of town."

Quickly I gave her my address and told her to write to me. I really didn't think I was likely to hear from her, but I did. We carried on a correspondence for several months as she moved from place to place. Time has clouded my memory of those letters. As I write this I find myself wishing I'd saved them but I did not. Once she told me she liked the house they were in, another time that she had a boyfriend, and finally the letters stopped.

Other children came into my classroom from time to time. I provided my daughter's outgrown clothes to one grateful little girl. To avoid embarrassing her at school I dropped them off at her house. The house was unkempt beyond any house I've ever been in, but both child and mother were glad to see me. Before long, she too was gone, and I never knew where.

One year several other teachers and I provided clothes for a boy. We told him they were my son's outgrown clothes—and some were—but we'd purchased others. That mother was irate and made him give them back.

I'd like to say that I changed students' lives, but most likely I did not. However, since the days of Joe Green, I came to see that even if I couldn't undo bad learning habits or change learning styles, at least I could make them feel comfortable for a time.

If you're still out there, Joe Green, I'd like you to know that I wish I'd been less demanding, less focused on books and more in tune with a boy who was never in one place long enough to make friends. I was young and inexperienced. Through the years I've thought about you and hoped that a few teachers came into your life, cared more about you as a person, less about learning habits, and did a better job than I.

**A Time
to Reflect**

Light Amid Darkness

It was tempting to make this book merely a collection of amusing and pensive recollections. But I feel compelled to include comments about a part of my life that has been difficult, not only for me, but also for family and friends who have shared my experiences in a continuing journey with mental illness. At one time I tried to pinpoint its beginnings. Not being able to do so, I concluded that the beginnings are really not important. The important thing is to find ways to deal with a reality I had once tried to deny. For much of my life I've experienced mood swings fluctuating from mild to profound, but settling from time to time at satisfying points between the poles.

I tried many different ways to make myself feel better: prayer and meditation, herbs, medical and chiropractic doctors, self-hypnosis tapes and self-help books. I reached for strength within myself, upward for strength outside myself, and lived in denial. In the mid-1980s my regular doctor diagnosed me as depressed and anxious. He gave me anti-depressants, which made me feel worse. After disposing of them, I told everyone I was suffering from exhaustion, and struggled on with my life.

In the early nineties, going on with my life became impossible. Professional counseling was my first option. Once my therapist told me she thought I was in a manic stage and should see a psychiatrist. For weeks I tried to pull myself out of it, but finally had to admit that she was right. By then, my moods were spiraling downward. The first psychiatrist I saw diagnosed me as major depressive recurrent. As it had been with my general practitioner, his prescriptions made me feel worse. After experimenting for several weeks, I disposed of them too. Then in April of 1992, I admitted myself to Charter Hospital in Sioux Falls, where I was diagnosed with bipolar disorder, a kinder name for manic-depressive illness.

The diagnosis was not surprising. I'd made jokes about being a closet manic-depressive for many years. It wasn't a shock to my husband or children either. They had witnessed my frequent mood swings, ranging from episodes of being totally incapacitated with depression to those of expansive energy, optimism and ambition.

Once Orv commented, "Sometimes you can move the world

and all its contents, and at other times the world and all its contents can't move you." His words, made out of frustration, remain the best description of my experiences with bipolar disorder that I have ever heard.

I regret that my children and grandchildren, as well as others, have been exposed to my unreasonable side more often than I care to remember. Living with a bipolar person is frustrating and confusing. Moving into a manic stage makes me feel exceptionally well, almost indomitable. I tend to take on responsibilities, which later become difficult to finish. Intellectually, I know the euphoria won't last, but when it happens, it seems that I will always be vigorous. At times the euphoria is controllable and works to my advantage, but at other times it escalates into something worse. I can be unreasonably angry, short-tempered, and in my worst times, spinning out of control.

Those episodes are followed by a predictable fall into depression, guilt, and inability to take care of the simplest tasks. For much of my life I've used my highs to accomplish as much as possible, so when the lows come, I don't have so much to do. Different incidents trigger episodes. I could detail happenings which have contributed to my illness, but having done that privately in therapy, I choose not to do so again in a public forum. Some of the prescriptions I've used are the same as those given for seizures. It took many years and many trials to find medications that work for me.

These days, an effective regimen of medications along with learning to avoid certain stressors makes it possible for me to live an almost normal life. Encouraging therapists, several different doctors, a stay in a hospital, understanding pastors, and other valued individuals too numerous to mention have enabled me to achieve a rather manageable state of mind. Still, as with other chronic illnesses, I know the disorder will not leave me completely.

Throughout the years I spent in therapy, I wrote extensive journal entries and shared them with several different therapists or with friends who were on journeys similar to mine. Sometimes I gleaned stones and mortar from those entries, and used them to construct poems or reflective essays. Then, having harvested something of value from the pages, I burned them, committing their contents to another realm.

Journal Journey

Cautious flames consume words gleaned
from visceral vaults, once shoved into drawers marked

DO NOT JAR---DO NOT OPEN---DO NOT READ
CONTENTS MAY BE EXPLOSIVE.

Yet holding tenuously to hands
of those who cared about my quest
I journeyed through darkened halls
into dim-lit regions of my soul.

Carefully approaching locked files
I tried first one combination, then another
until at last the contents mingled with my life's blood
connected with my pen
and spewed forth in words of green and black and blue.

Then with flickering flame and short blaze
I entrusted words to One
who reads through burning embers
and hears the softest supplications.

> *Kyrie, Kyrie Eleison**
> *Fill my empty soul with peace.*

*Keer'-ee-ey e-ley'-uh-sawn—A part of the liturgical worship service,
meaning Lord have mercy.

Rivers of Life

Those with webbed feet
move merrily through
the swim of life.

Perhaps the goose
is not so silly
and some ducks do well
apart from the row.

While I navigate in lurches
they move with grace
in streams of universal thought
unaware of snags and traps
or currents.

Winter Solstice
In memory of Susan Gramstad

The day is gray
wind-blown snow clings to my window.
On such days
I once explored mild slopes
on cross-country skis.
Camaraderie made trails easy
tasks intriguing, coldness less severe.

Without my skiing companion—
gone for seven winters now
slopes are solemn.
There is no hilarity
in falling down alone.

Now I watch grandsons
build snow people, fight snow wars.
Later we will warm ourselves
with chocolate, marshmallows
and freshly popped corn.

Filled with their excitement
I will try once more
to assess life's gains and losses
and wait to see the spring.

Sisters' Connections

I put flowers on Amy's grave last May, the grave of a sister I never knew. Our lives were separated by more than six years from her death to my birth. But biologically, I am as connected to her as I am to the siblings I grew up with, the ones I knew well.

Throughout her lifetime, my mother sometimes called me Amy, and I was sort of pleased about that error. I'd heard over and over again how good Amy had always been, and relished the connection.

Even as a child, I understood that memories of the deceased become more cherished after their departure. I secretly suspected there had been more to Amy than the stories my parents told, stories of her intelligence, sweetness, commitment to faith, and brave fight with diabetes.

Sometimes my mother would open a small cedar letterbox to show me hand-written penciled letters, sent from McKennan Hospital in Sioux Falls, South Dakota, where Amy was treated from time to time. The box also contained letters filled with longing and hope from our mother, who wanted to be with her ailing nine-year-old child, but also who needed to be home caring for three younger children.

McKennan was a relatively new and up-to-date hospital in 1928, staffed by the Presentation Sisters. Nano Nagel had founded their order in Ireland in 1718. During a time when it was illegal for Irish children to learn about Roman Catholicism, she and her followers held secret schools in the daytime and made late-night lantern visits to care for the sick. In 1880, a small group of Presentation Sisters was sent to Dakota Territory to teach Lakota children. As their numbers grew they established schools and hospitals. In 1911, with money donated by a local philanthropist, Helen McKennan, they founded a hospital in Sioux Falls.*

As part of their mission they cared for my sister, making her time away from home more bearable. At the outset of her final hospitalization, Amy was not particularly ill. Our mother was to have abdominal surgery, and it seemed to be a good time for Amy to go along. She would receive training to inject her own insulin shots while Mom recuperated. No one had considered how deeply our mother's post-operative condition would affect the sensitive child.

More than once, I heard my father say, "She looked like a shadow passed over her face when she saw her mother after the operation."

Amy became ill, worsened, slipped into a coma, and died before my mother was well enough to be out of bed. Dad left his distraught wife to make funeral arrangements, accompanied his deceased child back to Rushmore by train, offered reassurances to his other children in their grandparents' care, attended the funeral, then boarded the train to return to the hospital and grieve with his wife.

When my parents told those stories, they often mentioned the kindnesses of the Presentation Sisters, women who openly wept for my mother and the comatose child. Dad never forgot their concern, which eased a bit of the Catholic/Protestant distrust prevalent at the time.

McKennan Hospital changed and grew though the years. Now called Avera** McKennan, it ranks in the top 100 United Stares hospitals according to *Newsweek* magazine's annual report. Occasionally, I would drive past the grounds, pull over to one side or another, searching for some remnant of the original brick structure, but I never found any. Three of my grandchildren were born there, and each time I visited the huge facility, I speculated about the old hospital and assumed all had been swallowed up by progressive updates or perhaps met the wrecking ball.

Then in 2006 and 2007, I had two orthopedic surgeries there. During an orientation session before my first procedure, I asked the physical therapist if any of the original building still exists. She said that part of it is standing, but plans are being made to raze it eventually.

When I recounted the family story from the twenties, she was kind enough to wheel me to an area where I could see a courtyard and parts of the original brick structure not visible from the street. The sight stirred deep connections within me, connections to my parents and to Amy, as though they had smoothed my path, serving as some sort of presence to get me through a trying time. Mom's unhappy surgical experience in 1928, and Amy's many hapless journeys to the hospital while fighting a losing battle with diabetes became fresh and current, almost as if I had been present at the time.

Benedictine and Presentation Sisters are still an integral part of McKennan. They no longer provide the entire nursing staff, but minister to spiritual and psychological needs of the patients.

On my registration form, I identified myself as Lutheran. A kind and helpful Protestant chaplain, rather than the Sisters, called on me. I valued his calls, but perhaps my experience would have been enhanced if I had also visited with some of those women.

After my last surgery, I mentioned my feelings of connectedness to my niece Carol. She commented, "I can envision that somewhere in a retirement home, there is an ancient nun who was a young nurse when Grandma and Amy were there. Perhaps on some level she feels blessed for having known them."

I like to imagine that elusive woman who may have been moved by their faith, just as her faith moved my father. Perhaps the Protestant/Catholic differences also mattered a little less to her.

In March of 2009, I made another connection. While at McKennan undergoing further tests for continuing issues with the way I walk, I asked for more information about the old hospital. Someone pointed out a rather large section, which still exists. I was told to take the elevator to the third floor to get into the part of the old hospital. It was a bit of a disappointment as the interior looked like any other part of the hospital. The doors, windows and floors have all been updated. When I stopped at a nurses' station to inquire if any part of the old hospital might be original, one of the nurses directed me to the stairwell.

There I found a gray terrazzo staircase with oak railings on either side. Hesitantly, I decided it would be worth the trouble to walk down those steps, the same ones my father must have used when he visited his wife and child. The difficulties with my gait did not diminish the strong sibling connection with the sister I never knew, as I keyed in on a deep level with the realities of what my parents had experienced. How does one explain connections or the need to find them?

Women with Vision: The Presentation Sisters of South Dakota, 1880-1985, by Susan Carol Petersen, Courtney Ann Vaughn-Roberson, Published by university Press, 1988.

**In need of atonement.*

***Nano Nagel passed on her guiding principle to the members of the order, "Love another as you have hitherto done."

Letting Go, Part One

I let go of my mother's hand
at the county fair.
Overwhelmed with panic
amid a crowd of strangers
until with watchful eyes
she reached down
to touch my hand.

She had strong hands, capable
of much, including
holding on too tightly
but those hands held comfort
truth, integrity and me.

I held her hand one last time
in a candle-lit death watch
on a warm July night in 1964
as she let go of life.

Sometimes, overwhelmed
with panic in crowds
of strange emotions
I see her watchful eyes
and feel her touch my hand again.

Letting Go, Part Two

I let go of
six baby kittens
furry bodies
mangled in the hay.

The crime, not witnessed
but Rex slunk away
guilt as real as the tail
between his legs.

I'd ignored him
loving the kittens far too much
not dreaming he'd
carry jealousy so far.

We never were the same again
Rex and I
both filled with guilt
both lacking the capacity
of letting go.

Letting Go, Part Three

I thought our lives could be cut clean
separated with surgical steel.
Yet memories of past indignities
had collected beneath the surface—
a giant hematoma
which broke the poorly
stitched incision and gushed forth
leaving a gaping wound.

At last it healed
leaving a hard yet tender scar
which I attempted to conceal
with counterfeit smiles and laughter.

And I conceal it still
a near-forgotten thing
until climatic changes
bring it to mind again
causing me to stumble a bit
before I catch my breath
and then move on.

The Woman at the Well

I was leaving the labyrinth for the second time on the last day of the retreat when I heard the harp music. I planned to stop at the recreation center to shower before the dinner bell would ring at the farmhouse, to prepare for leave-taking and a four-hour drive home. At first it seemed that I was fantasizing the music, but as I left the field I knew that it was real and tried to identify its source.

Clare's Well is a retreat center near Annandale, Minnesota, operated by Franciscan Nuns. A good friend had recommended the place to me for healing and restoration. I had arrived four days before, seeking a quiet place to calm my thoughts and gain perspective on life's many transitions. Nothing was required of me as a guest, except to draw from my own well of spiritual understanding.

The retreat consists of a farmhouse, a barn, a garage, a recreation center, and three hermitages. The smallest hermitage accommodates one person; another, two; and the larger one, three. There is also a room for one person to stay in the farmhouse, which is the home of three nuns in blue jeans, T-shirts, and walking shoes. I chose to stay in the farmhouse room.

The Sisters raise an organic garden, tend goats, chickens, guineas and other fowl, do massage, keep up the house and grounds, and cook outstanding meals for the guests.

I used the retreat's extensive collection of books and CDs to appreciate music and read. I also read from my own books, wrote in my journal, spent time in the hot tub, experienced two types of massage, visited with the Sisters and other guests at mealtime, and soaked up hours alone with my thoughts.

I knew about using a labyrinth as a tool for centering the self. I have seen more elaborate labyrinths lined with stones and with benches for sitting and contemplation.

But the labyrinth at Clare's Well is a continuous rounding path with switchbacks, simply mowed in the middle of a field recently sown with native flowers and grasses. I was told of the value of moving to the center for prayer, meditation, and focusing. For me the centering came from the crunch of the stubble beneath my feet, listening to the birds, watching the guinea fowl move at my approach, and seeing the women work efficiently about the buildings and in the garden. It took me back to familiar sounds and sights of my childhood when belief in the goodness of God, family, community, and country was innocent and untried.

That crunch also resurrected visions of times my mother sent me to the fields with lemonade or water for my father. Mom was afraid he was working too hard in the heat of the hot summer days, and wanted to be sure Dad had enough to drink so as not to become dehydrated by the power of the sun. She never seemed to think about the fact that she was cooking on a wood stove in a hot kitchen, facing heat with no cooling breezes, and since we had no electricity, there was not even a fan.

I walked the labyrinth twice each day. On that fourth day, the crunch of the stubble beneath my feet reminded me that beliefs, tempered by life, are even more valued than untried ideals of a child. That was when I heard the harp.

As I approached the farmhouse I saw a woman sitting in an unusual chair beside a picnic bench. She was playing a lap harp. I assumed that her presence was part of the plan of the retreat, and went closer to listen. She wore braces on her legs, and sat in a chair with wheels, more simple than a regular wheel chair. She and a friend were enjoying the day with a blue cloudless sky and rural surroundings. I sat down on the bench beside her to listen and to visit. They were pleasant, articulate women who had driven the thirty miles or so from Minneapolis, and were out enjoying the morning. They'd heard of Clare's Well, and came not to stay or eat, but just to see the farm place. It was their first visit.

The woman with the lap harp told me that she often carries the instrument with her when she visits hospitals or friends' homes, and plays it to comfort and to entertain. The music was lovely, otherworldly. I told her how I have always loved harp music. She handed the instrument to me and directed me to put it on my lap. Having no gift for music except for listening, I was reluctant, but she insisted that I take it.

"Just run your fingers over the strings," she instructed. "You can't make a bad sound on the harp"

Hesitantly, I did as she said, and was delighted to learn that she was right. You can't make a bad sound on the harp. I held the instrument briefly before giving it back to her. Then, encouraged by her openness, I asked her about the chair and the braces.

"I deal with post-polio problems," she said, "and I seemed to fall a lot. Then last year I had to have a hip replacement and the doctor told me I must not fall again."

I listened to her story with interest as she continued. "Since then," she went on, "I've learned to accept the graciousness of friends, and not be too proud to accept it. I take an arm when someone offers it to me while I cross the street, accept friends' offers to take me on drives like today, and use this chair in my house so I don't fall. I've learned to have respect for my handicap."

I'd drawn from my own well while on retreat, and learned much from people I'd neither met before nor expected to see again. I knew as I left the labyrinth for the last time, that the nuns, who had not instructed me at all, had taught me so much. Then, just before sitting down to the dinner table for the last time before driving home, I'd been gifted with music from the harp and the insight of a woman whose name I've forgotten.

I went to the retreat to deal with my own issues, followed rounded paths with switchbacks in the labyrinth—and in my mind. I felt more peace, though nothing in my life was really changed, nor had any conflicts been resolved. In the last hours of a four-day experience, the woman with the harp had summed it all up. I left Clare's Well with more respect for my own issues, my own journey, and my own many handicaps.

Lakeside Observations

Wind broken aspen arm
reaches to Mother Earth
its root source.
Upheld by maple thickets
sap rises then falls
nourished leaves
hold on.

Yellow dotted dandies
short glory days
white puffs
naked stems.

Jet trails
interrupt cloudless skies
mirrored in speed-boat's wake.

A View from the Hospital Window

A sheet of newsprint
gamboled in the grass
crumpled, misshapen.

Pages not yet faded by the sun
held messages of news, weather
and perhaps comics to initiate a laugh.

Separated by closed doors
and locked windows
she was too distant
too full of her own thoughts
to care for more messages
she could not quite decipher.

Monarch

The fragile King of the Butterflies
carries no luggage
trusts loyal subjects
to sustain his journey.

The Parking Lot

Tar and concrete
seek to obliterate the prairies.
Here and there, steadfast violets
in flaws and fissures
raise miniscule heads
and proudly fight back.

Moonlight Madness

There is a world owned by insomniacs
with realities they'd not choose to know.
Their spirits, worn, but active minds still lack
ability to let confusion go.
They see the rising of the moon and sun
and agonize for missteps from the past
arise to do some day chores left undone
seek calm by bending to some muted task.

They try to smile when others rise refreshed
and face the new day with a firm resolve
hoping some night they too can be so blessed
with peaceful sleep and all their worries solved.

They go about the day just feeling zapped
and seek a time and place to take a nap.

Sonnet to a Prairie Rose

Rose was born in eighteen eighty-nine
the year Dakota's statehoods first were claimed.
She played in fields of blooming columbine
and soft pink prairie rose, for which she's named.
She was raised to be a lady, sweet and kind
to wait for life to bless her as it should.
And as John's wife, she never seemed to mind
living life the way he wished she would.

Rose lived her whole life near the prairie sod
loved her home, her children, and her friends.
Her heart was always very close to God
so she was well prepared to meet him in the end.

She cherished comely prairie flowers and grasses
so gladly they at last received her ashes.

Seventh Sister of the Pleiades

The Ancients starred her nights with mythic view
filled with magnificence and golden hue.
She gamboled through the skies—a loose ellipse
till Atlas saved her from Orion's grip.

Cepheus ignored her—proud Egyptian king.
She fantasized about a Saturn ring
when Ursa Minor with dim dignity
enamored her with his polarity.

He saw her—no miniscule reflection—
with muted light entirely her own
visible, not worthy of rejection
he had telescopic vision and she shone.

Though she was veiled, he heard her muffled shout
Hey, look at me—my light is not snuffed out.

Downcast/Uplifted

I was swept away by waters flowing
consumed by rising, overwhelming tides
faltered while my inner fears were growing
at sea, where swelling waves would not subside.

Reaching out for comfort from someone at my side
seemed a grim, impossible endeavor
a descent into helpless ride
with my future spiritless forever.

Then something lights the dark to sever
melancholy doldrums from my mind
driving fears so far it seems they'll never
invade my heart and soul another time.

Still—at times for some mysterious reason
they descend to haunt me for a season.

Isaiah 43:2-3—When you pass through deep waters, I am with you.
When you pass through rivers, they will not sweep you away.
Walk through flames and they will not burn you.

The Mayo Clinic Experience—1989

Evening, East on I-90

Behind me a golden sun slips from view
while shades of winter mauves and grays
color my rear-view mirror.
Hues turn to darkness
my world shrinks to the breadth
and span of my headlights.

Approaching vehicles dim their lights
across the median and three lanes away.
Dusk to dawn lights
and the iridescence of an approaching town
give evidence of a world larger
than the scope of head-light distance.

Before me a cone-shaped light
behind murky clouds
offers a promise of a full moon later on.

On the left, the Blue Earth radio tower
suddenly announces

J
E
S
U
S

I
S

L
O
R
D

in red lights.

Over Super America
at the Waseca exit
a neon roadrunner runs continuously
to the beat of Rachmaninoff
on Minnesota Public Radio.

Clouds thin
the cone-shaped light spreads
a golden moon slips into view
relieving shades of black and gray.
The eastern sky glows, the road lightens
my vision expands
beyond the boundaries of my lights.

Man and the Energies

On a couch too short
to accommodate his length, he lay
with face pained, arthritic legs bent.
His bibbed overalls and western boots
in sharp contrast to the wall mural
Man and the Energies.

I've had my tests, Jim
let's go home.

A younger version of himself
lithe legs bent, in Levis and western boots
leaned forward easily in his plastic chair.

More tests to come, Pop
everyone waits at Mayo.

I'm glad you're here, Son
I'd be lost in this place without you.

I'm glad I'm here too, Pop.

Sympathetic eyes turned momentarily to the pair
then focused on their own appointments
their own waiting, their own pain.

Under a Winter Moon

A thin young man
hardly more than a boy
stood at my door
on a cold, snowy night
in early December.

He carried wind chimes
with moons and stars
and wore a badge identifying
him as Russian
a member of
the Unification Church.

Are you with Sun Myung Moon
I queried.

Reverend Moon very good man
he said in halting English.

I warned my grandchildren
my neighbors
the clergy
about cults in our home town.

But still on cold nights
a thin boy and his Russian
mother haunt my thoughts.
While she wonders about her
cold, underfed son
she doesn't know
this Iowa mother
turned him away
without so much as a sandwich.

Generations Come and Generations Go

But The Earth Abides Forever. Ecc. 1:4

Sehnsucht

According to my Uncle John Hembd, now deceased, the following is a poem written during the 1880s by my grandmother, Anna Elizabeth Hembd. She wrote this poem after three of her children had found employment far away from home. In some of the verses she seems to be mourning for someone who has died. That tone is understandable; as she had already buried five of the nineteen children she bore.

The late Christine Peters of Hartley, Iowa translated the original text for me, and I did my best to put my grandmother's thoughts into English verse, using her rhythm and rhyming pattern. However, you will notice a variation in the length of the two pieces.

Christine told me many years ago that there is no real English equivalent to the word Sehnsucht. My current research on the Internet agrees with that assessment. According to Wikipedia it is a deeply intense and inconsolable longing. Because of this information I have kept my grandmother's German title for the English translation.

I would like to thank Rev. Francis Mennenga and Brigitte Green for providing me with a thorough and expanded translation of the poem, as well as checking the spelling and adding the umlauts.

Sehnsucht

by Anna Elizabeth Hembd, circa 1880

Sag´ ,was ist´s , was meine Seele
Bis im tiefsten Grund durchzieht,
Dass sie wie aus dunkler Höhle
Aufzuschweben sich bemüht?

Was ist´s, was das Herz erzittern,
Tief im Grund erbeben lässt,
Wie ein Sturm in Ungewittern,
Der da beugt die starken Äst?

Ja, was macht das Herze zagen,
Wenn die Lieben von uns gehen,
Dass wir uns dann ängstlich fragen,
Ob wir sie auch wiedersehen?

Ach, was fühlt da das Gemüthe?
Ist´s nicht für das arme Herze
Wie ein Frost auf junger Blüte;
Ist das nicht Sehnsucht-Schmerz?

Ach, es ist hier nichts vollkommen:
Wahres Glück währt kurze Zeit;
Dann wird´s wieder aufgenommen,*
Und es folgt die Traurigkeit;

Das Kind, das dir so weit hinaus,
Es sieht in die Welt hinaus.
Du bleibst zurück mit deinen Schmerzen
Und leer und öde wird das Haus.

Aber du musst nicht verzagen,
Und nicht so betrübet sein;
Denn es folgen schönere Tage,
Und nach Regen Sonnenschein.

Ja, es gibt ein Wiedersehen,
Was das Herz mit Freude füllt.
Dann erst wirst du recht verstehen,
Wie dir Gott die Sehnsucht stillt.

*Translator commented that this line does not seem to be quite right.

Sehnsucht

Why do I find my soul
in earth's deepest darkest depths?
I try softly to escape its caverns
and find some inner rest.

What makes my heart to flutter
in earth's caverns all shut in
tossed about in storms so mighty
that will bend the strongest limb?

Yes, what will the heart utter
when our loved ones go away
when we scarcely dare to question
will we meet again one day?

Oh, what is this deep emotion?
It's not for the impoverished of heart
it's as the frost upon the flower bud
it is the pain when they depart.

A child you love with all your heart
leaves for another sphere
and you stay home in sorrow—
oh, the house seems empty here.

Spirit, don't give up and don't feel sad
sunshine will follow after rain.
There will be better days ahead of us
and we will meet again.

Then our hearts will swell with happiness
and we will understand
how God takes of loneliness
with his tender, loving hand.

Grandmother Anna Elizabeth

She was a lover of poetry and people
schooled in the methods of healing
in her day.

She knew how to make an ointment
from elderberry leaves
to soothe reddened, aching eyes
or how to moisten bread with milk
to draw the pain
from an infected finger.

She knew, too, how to use
the ointment of her faith
to soothe the lives
of nineteen children
and filled their souls
with enough joy and laughter
to endure for nineteen lifetimes
of various spans.

But I know her by reputation only—
our lives were parted by a gap
of twenty-one years
from her death to my birth.

But I have sought her
in the memories of her children
and I know a part of her survives in me—
a portion of what I am.

And once I sought her
in a distant Minnesota cemetery
and put wild flowers
on her grave.

The original of the following was among papers my parents saved. Dad wrote it when he was a student at The University of Southern Minnesota in Austin, Minnesota in about 1916. His grade was A, Excellent.

The Old Home
By Herman Hembd

If you were to have a vacation to spend wherever you wish some of you would perhaps go to some city where you could go to dances, theatres, or other places of amusement. Others might prefer going to see the great wide ocean, which you have heard so much about. Some one of you may have a very dear friend somewhere, with whom you would like to spend your vacation.

Let me tell you where I spent my vacation last summer. I spent my vacation in my old home country in the hills; the home of my childhood days; the most beautiful place on earth. Of course you may disagree with me in the last statement; that is because you were not born and raised there.

I want to tell you some things about my home country and I think I can do so best by telling you of my visit there last June.

I left Austin on the Milwaukee Road going east to the Mississippi River. I changed cars at La Crescent, a small town a short distance from the river, and went south between the river and a row of hills, which run perpendicular to the river. The minute I saw the old river, a peaceful feeling came stealing over me. It brought back old memories that had almost been forgotten. I thought of the happy times I had in my younger days boating, fishing, and swimming in that same old river.

After having gazed up the river for about ten minutes I took a seat on the other side of the car. Lazily leaning back and gazing at the high, steep wooded hills, I became as one in a dream. I dreamt of the days of my childhood with the work about the home, to great pleasure in climbing to the top of one of these high hills, walking as near as we dared, to the end toward the river to look down on the objects below.

At the bottom were tall straight black oaks, perhaps almost one hundred feet high. From where we stood they looked to be nothing more than tall weeds. But there was another sight more interesting, perhaps. It was a long freight train coming down the long valley. Winding its way down the track with its many curves and turns, it looked like a large snake picking its way through the grass.

We could not stand long on the end of this cliff and look down, for it seemed like there was a strong magnet at the bottom drawing us down. Imagine yourself on the roof of a twenty-story building, facing the roof of another twenty-story building, looking on the street below, and you will have an idea of what it is to stand at the edge of a cliff from three to six hundred feet high.

After we were tired of looking down from our high perch, we might walk back on the top of the hill until we would strike a road leading to the valley below; but more likely we would pick our way down the steep side of the hill. We never failed to find large stones to roll on ahead of us. It was great sport to see them start, rather slowly at first, then gaining speed, strike a tree now and then, bounce to one side and roll on. Some of these stones might find their way to the bottom by rolling, bounding, striking trees, jumping and rolling some more. Others might make a good start, strike a tree, bound back and start over only to find another tree or stump in its path, which would bring it to a stop.

I did not have long to dream about these things, for I soon heard the brakeman yell, "Brownsville," and I knew that it was time to get off. I was not slow in getting off the train for I already saw familiar faces. I was quite busy for some time shaking the hands of old friends who happened to be at the depot or on the street.

As Brownsville has no longer a home for me I intended going to the hotel, but I found old friends who soon made me change my plans. I received a hearty welcome wherever I went.

After having enjoyed the company of old friends I decided to have at least a few days to myself, to visit the old haunts of my childhood.

As I walked across the meadows to the old swimming hole, it seemed I never before saw such beautiful grass, or heard the birds sing so sweetly. Even the willow brush around the swimming hole looked beautiful to me.

I found that the old swimming hole had not changed much, except that in a few places it was a little deeper and in other places it was filled in with dirt and sand.

After a good refreshing bath I picked my way up a steep side hill. After reaching the top I soon found the place on the warm south end where we always found our first crocuses in the early spring.

From the end of this hill, I had a good view of the village with the river on the east of it. It was a most beautiful sight. A large steamboat was going down the river pushing a long raft of logs ahead of it. Another boat, which looked like an excursion boat, was plowing its way upstream, several row boats and gasoline launches were going in various directions, not seeming to care much where they were headed. They were, no doubt occupied by fishers or pleasure seekers.

After feasting my eyes on the beautiful sights to be seen from this place, I found a cow path leading to the other side of the hill. I followed the path and it led me almost directly to the place where I wanted to go. It was an almost level spot a little over half way to the foot of the hill. Here were some weeds and tall ferns, but that was not what I was looking for.

This was the place we used to call "the flower patch." Many kinds of flowers might have been found here a few weeks earlier. Most of them grew just above the little flat on the steep rocky side hill. However, on the flat we found the honeysuckle and also the lady's slipper.

By walking around I managed to find a few half-withered flowers of various kinds. Even though they were withered they were very dear to me, for they brought back sweet memories of happy days.

On my way back to the village I chose a path that led me to an old meadow. In this meadow were small hills, but quite steep, in fact too steep to drive on with machinery. For this reason they were sowed to grass. Some years this grass was cut with a scythe and other years it was not cut at all, depending on the crop of grass it raised. It was mostly June grass and stood quite thin.

As I walked down the side of one of these little knolls I found what I was looking for. Here were great patches of nice, red wild strawberries, just as I saw them years ago. I filled my hat and hurried home. It was already a few minutes past twelve, and I had worked up a good appetite.

After eating a hearty dinner I took a pole and line and visited our old fishing place. Some of the old stumps and stones that we used to sit on when I was a boy were still there. As this was not a good fishing season I did not make a big catch, however I was lucky enough to bring out a few bass, one small catfish and several sunfish.

After rowing for some time and having another bath, I went home feeling better for having seen some of the old familiar places.

In the last days of June and the beginning of July, I spent most of my time out in the woods, on stony hillsides, along line fences, and at the edge of big ditches, picking raspberries. They could be found most any place where the ground was not disturbed by the stock or by the plow. I did not pick the berries, as much for the berries as for the sake of doing something that I used to do when I was a boy.

It seemed to be a good year for wild fruit, for the grape vines, which could be seen most any place in the woods, as well as the wild plum trees which were heavily loaded with fruit. The cherry trees and gooseberry bushes seemed to be taking a rest for they had few berries on their branches.

Now, that you may not get the impression that only wild fruit is found there, let me tell you, all the fruit mentioned besides a few kinds not mentioned may also be found on the farms and in the gardens where it grows much larger.

I could have spent the whole summer at Brownsville and would have enjoyed it very much, but my vacation was coming to an end, and there was another place that I must visit before going back to my work. It was an old country home about seven miles southwest of Brownsville. That is where I was born and lived until I was six years old.

I hitched up a team early one morning and drove out there. The old place was deserted and most of the buildings had collapsed. In fact the place looked rather strange to me at first. As I tied my team to the stump of an old plum tree and walked up to the remains of the old log house, I felt as though I was walking on sacred ground. For this was my first home; the home in which I knew nothing of this big world; the home wherein I knew no sorrow, sin, or wrong.

I spent several hours there looking the old place over. I knew just where the garden had been; where each building had stood; it all came back to me as a dream.

The old hickory tree just north of the house was still standing, and although it was partly dried some of the branches were loaded with nuts, which were about half grown. Several of the apple trees and plum trees were still green and bearing fruit.

As I was looking things over, there came to my mind the old "play house," as we called it out in the woods about forty rods north of the house, and I set out at once to see if I could find the place.

As I walked through the forest of big oaks, some of which are perhaps several hundred years old, I saw many familiar places. I even recognized some of the old trees. It was like meeting old friends.

I had no trouble in finding our old "play house." The stones that my older brothers and sisters had piled up years ago were still there. I also found old, rusty iron kettles and pieces of dishes, which we had carried there. I sat there for at least an hour thinking of the happy days spent there years ago.

After my vacation was over, I was almost certain that I never will find another home on this earth that can be as dear to me as my first home, the home of my childhood days.

Grandma's Living Legacy

My maternal grandmother nurtured a special plant with wide, deep-green leaves. It flourished among the ferns, coleus, and African violets. Sometimes a stalk or two would shoot up among the leaves, bud, then blossom into five to seven perfect white lilies. They were star shaped and about four inches in diameter.

According to family legend, the original bulbs from that plant came to this country with the Howes, an immigrant family, in the mid 1800s. Their daughter Bertha, who was to become my grandmother, was twelve years old at the time. She journeyed with her parents and three siblings on a sailing ship from Germany to America. Among their possessions were the carefully packed parent bulbs of the lily in Grandma's window. They would provide my great-grandmother with ties to the home they were leaving.

Once a storm beat and tossed the ship, frightening all. Young Bertha feared they would all drown, and the money, carefully saved for the trip, would have been wasted. Fortunately, the passengers survived the storm and so did the bulbs.

After my grandmother's death, my mother and her sister Freda divided the plant between them. Mom was a warm and giving person, but she did not have the knack for raising that particular plant, and hers did not thrive, so she decided to give her bulbs with their dwindling leaves to her sister.

It was Aunt Freda who told me the stories of the ocean voyage when she went to live in a care center, and she entrusted those historic bulbs to me. I nurtured them as well as I could, but they never looked as healthy as they did in Grandma's or Aunt Freda's houses.

Following Mom's example, I gave part of the bulbs to my sister. Marge has a home with healthy, verdant plants in an east bay window. Under her care the plant blossomed, and its bulbs multiplied so prolifically that she had to divide them. She re-potted some to give away to others. My portion dwindled and paled.

Through the years, Marge distributed plants to her daughters and daughters-in-law, our sister Esther, nieces, nephews, and cousins. She even gave some back to me because mine were pale, thin, and spindly. She also potted some for her church, and those flourished too. The offspring of Grandma's lily are now lush and green in the homes of relatives in Iowa, Minnesota, South Dakota, California, and Texas.

Embarrassed by my own poor effort, I asked others for advice. One sister-in-law told me to put the bulbs into a new pot and use new potting soil. Now my flowerpot boasts eight long, wide, healthy, deep-green leaves. I have been waiting for stalks to shoot up with buds that turn to blossoms of three or four perfect white lilies, but that never seems to happen.*

A few years ago my husband and I were going to visit relatives in Texas. Marge sent a flowerpot containing bulbs and leaves from Grandma's lily with us. They were for our nieces Peggy and Paula who live in Houston. Marge apologized for the gift, saying that particular plant never bloomed, but it was the only one she could spare at the time. About two months after our vacation ended, Paula e-mailed a picture of the plant with several of those lovely white blossoms. Perhaps they just needed a change of scenery.

I saw a plant just like Grandma's in a flower shop once and asked the florist for its name. She called it a Eucharist lily. I like that name. It denotes the almost sacred living legacy handed down through the generations. I'd like to believe the story of the bulbs on shipboard, but research makes me doubtful. I learned that the plant originated in South America, and its other name is Amazon lily. It occurs to me that the idea of those bulbs coming from Germany, in the mid-nineteenth century, is a bit of a stretch.

I can be certain of their history only since the 1940s. Still, through those plants, generations of Howe relatives have found a sort of mystical connection. We value our grandmother's and aunt's vision in preserving the plants for themselves in order to pass them along to other generations. I carry a rather embarrassed pride that my mother and I could see that our portions of the legacy needed to be given away in order to flourish. I continue to be amazed that my sister's care would be the impetus for the bulbs to become prolific enough to be shared with others while she is around to enjoy the pleasure.

At family gatherings we often discuss the state of our lilies. We know whose will bloom and whose will not. We discuss the numbers of our leaves and who has been able to divide the bulbs and give some away. The plants enrich our connections with each other as well as with those who have gone on before. Grandma, Mom, and Aunt Freda would all be pleased and amused if they could hear our stories. I'm sure they would find satisfaction in

Marge's generosity of spirit in passing bulbs on. Even if our great-grandmother really had no connection to our plants, it's nice to have her as part of the family lore. Her difficult voyage and life are remembered and honored by descendents who never knew her.

The winter of 2009 and 2010 was harsh and cold. I was dealing with the discomfort from orthopedic issues. Then on a February morning, about the time I sent the manuscript for The Earth Abides to the editor, I was delighted to notice a budding stalk shooting up among the leaves. I enjoyed the buds as much as I treasured the blossoms that followed. They seemed to deliver a message from Grandma reminding me that winter wouldn't last forever.

Mother's Oblations

Her day was graced
with the sacramental wine
of soapy water cut with lye
to cleanse the souls of family clothing.

She sorted impure whites from darker hues
commingling the crisply new
with those more worn and shabby
cleansing all.

Smudged white penitents
baptized in boiling water over fires
stoked with cobs and hickory kindling
lost their guilty stains.

Her red hands
refined by the ordinary
offered up our garments
to full exposure of the sun.

Blessed in fresh, clean nightclothes
we breathed in the air of thankfulness
beneath sheets which smelled as good
as tomorrow's fresh bread.

Life and Death Connections

A stately gray stone, partly hewn, partly polished, stands in a small cemetery near Rushmore, Minnesota. It is inscribed with the name *ROSENBERG*. My earliest connections with grief were observed there, rather than experienced.

In 1916, my grandfather purchased a lot in that cemetery, and two stones. The more imposing one, with the Rosenberg name, still presides over a lot large enough for ten graves. The smaller headstone was for his youngest child, nineteen-year-old Mable.

She was my mother's sister and roommate at a small university in Austin, Minnesota. When Mable became ill with tonsillitis, the two sisters, accompanied by Herman Hembd, the man who was to become my father, rode a steam-powered train back to Rushmore. Mable needed her own home and her mother's care, but she died within a week after that train ride, leaving a lifetime of grief for many.

In 1920, Uncle Ed and Aunt Clara added another small headstone, simply marked Infant, for their stillborn child. My own parents added the third in 1928 for their first-born child, little Amy Hembd. She had succumbed to diabetes just short of her tenth birthday. I came along in 1934 and grew up listening to poignant stories of those early deaths, fascinated with the oral family histories.

On May 30th of each year, we observed what was then called Decoration Day. I went with my parents, sisters, grandmother, and aunt to the cemetery. The women gathered irises, peonies, and lilacs from their own bushes and flowerbeds and used green Mason canning jars for vases. My sister, Esther, and I filled those jars from the Dempster Mill Pump half way down a gentle slope, and the women decorated the graves. Each visit was a somber adventure. My grandmother and aunt were grim and stoic, but I became accustomed to seeing tears in my mother's eyes; tears which reappeared every time Amy's name was mentioned, for as long as my mother lived.

The ten-grave cemetery plot is almost full now. My grandparents, Uncles Carl and Ed, Aunt Clara, and Cousin Raymond, who died of rheumatic fever at age 16, now have headstones similar to the original three I remember from childhood. One place is vacant and will remain so. My parents and other family members were interred in other cemeteries.

Sometimes I visit the Rushmore cemetery and place flowers in the Rosenberg plot, but I always leave with the feeling that irises, peonies, and lilacs would have been better. Maybe some year I'll ignore that last Monday of May, which we now call Memorial Day. I think next year on May 30th I'll observe Decoration Day with appropriate flowers. I could put them in green Mason canning jars, fill them with water from the old Dempster Mill Pump, and leave one on Amy's grave and another beside that stately gray stone.

Stars in the Window

Whenever we had a family picture taken between 1941 and 1945, my mother would insist that we stand outside under the big double windows so the flags could be in the picture too. The United States government supplied the families of service men and women with flags as symbols of those in uniform. Two such flags hung in our farmhouse in a little Iowa town called Ocheyedan.

One had a single star with a golden fringe. It was an overseas flag representing my oldest brother, Bob. He was serving a one-year tour of duty with the National Guard beginning in March of 1941. His year was three-fourths over when the Japanese bombed Pearl Harbor, and the country was at war. After the United States declared war on Japan, Germany and Italy declared war on the United States. Tours of duty became quickly changed and classified, "for the duration of the War plus six months."

At age six, much of what was occurring in the world was unclear and mysterious to me. My parents spoke about the war in serious, hushed tones and speculated about where Bob would be sent. During the next years his letters often arrived with large sections inked out or cut out, and a New York postmark. My mother said that meant he was in the European theater of the war.

His tour of duty led him to Ireland, Africa, and Italy, serving under Generals George Patton and Mark Clark. When he was moved from one place to another his letters would come postmarked, "Somewhere in . . ." My worried parents predicted where he might be going. They were always right and I could not figure out how they knew. Edward R. Murrow's broadcasts and Ernie Pyle's columns were relatively unknown to me.

The flag in the other window had two stars. It didn't have a golden fringe because the ones it represented were not outside the United States. One star stood for my brother Arnold, and the other for his wife, Bonnie. Arnold was drafted after the conflict began. He was trained to take code as a radio operator in the newly formed Army Air Force. Arnold was naturally left-handed, and often talked about the confusion he felt as regulations required that he tap out codes with his right hand.

He was stationed in several places from Florida to California, and for a while, he was stationed at the air base in Sioux Falls, just 65 miles from home. He came home frequently when he had a weekend pass. During the time he was in Sioux Falls he married Bonnie, his hometown sweetheart. She had been a schoolteacher but decided that if her husband were to be in the service, she would be too. She joined the WAVES and wore her uniform with pride. She trained and served as an airplane mechanic. I was the only one in my grade who had a sister-in-law and I was proud of her being in the service and being a mechanic to boot. Later they were both stationed near San Francisco, and could spend weekend passes together.

My parents worried a lot about Arnold being in California because they knew he might be sent somewhere in the Pacific. Their opinions were that the Pacific was even worse than Europe; that we did not understand the Oriental mind when it came to fighting wars, and such diseases as malaria, jungle rot, or yellow fever awaited Arnold if he should be sent overseas. Miraculously, he never had to go.

My most disturbing childhood memory is of coming home from school to find my mother weeping. She would be holding a letter from someone whose only presence was represented by a star in the window.

My father's family wrote a "round robin," a collection of letters sent from one family to another among the eleven living siblings, who were scattered across the country from Wisconsin to California. When the letters arrived at our house we read them thoroughly; then my father would take out his previous letter, add a new one and send the "robin" on its way. I began to know aunts and uncles scattered from Wisconsin to California though I had never met them in person. Among the letters there were pictures of cousins in uniform, perhaps twenty or more, and I was proud of them all.

Years later I began to comprehend the dangers they had faced and the marvel that not one of them was killed or seriously wounded. Once Bob received a surface wound from a piece of shrapnel, but refused the Purple Heart because he didn't want to worry my parents. One cousin came home from the Philippines with malaria, and my state-bound brother dealt with a foot that was not properly cared for after a service-connected injury, but there were no physical war casualties.

Those were days of heart-felt patriotism with flag waving, ration stamps, and War Bonds. I used to save dimes and nickels to buy twenty-five cent stamps to put in a book. When I had $18.75 worth of stamps, I could trade the book for a bond that would be worth $25 in ten years. Recycling was a national passion. We saved tinfoil from gum wrappers, washed and crushed tin cans, collected milkweed pods for life jackets, and planted victory gardens. My favorite aunt worked in a defense plant in Minneapolis.

Marijuana, which had been eradicated from road ditches, was reintroduced and renamed hemp. Its fibers were used for the manufacture of rope and twine, since the import of sisal from other countries was hampered by the war. Hogs noted for their fat were in demand as the lard was used in the manufacture of munitions.

Gasoline and tire rationing dictated that family outings were infrequent and a bit of an endurance test. The speed limit was 35 miles per hour, which almost everyone observed, as the slower speed saved gas and tires. Twice a year we went to Lake Okoboji, twenty-five miles from home. One time was for the Sunday-School picnic and the other was for the Farm Bureau picnic. On the way home we might pick up hitchhiking soldiers and take them as far as Ocheyedan where they hoped to pick up other rides to get them back to the Sioux Falls Airbase. I am certain that my parents would have been leery of hitchhikers before and after the war, but the situation was different. It might have been one of their boys.

On Saturday nights the neighbors gathered in town to buy groceries, get haircuts, fill cars with gas, and visit. During that time my mother, with a group of Red Cross volunteers, folded bandages for servicemen.* Sometimes there were free movies shown outside in a vacant lot beside our new town hall that had been built by WPA workers just before the war. The lumberyard provided planks and cement blocks for seating at that outdoor theater.

Besides gas and tires, many other things were in short supply. We needed ration stamps for such things as coffee, sugar, and shoes. Like all of our neighbors who had just survived the Depression, my parents didn't regard the stamps as an impossible hardship.

During those years I received my greatest lesson in honesty. Each member of the family was allowed enough stamps to buy two pairs of shoes annually. Once my mother took me to buy a pair of shoes. After we left the store she discovered that the clerk had forgotten to ask for her ration stamp. Without a moment's hesitation she went back into the store and gave the stamp to the startled clerk. To this day I can never keep an extra nickel if someone gives me too much change. I can still see my mother with that ration stamp.

Having an airbase so close provided a special treat for students in our little rural school. Often the pilots would fly in formation overhead. When we heard them, we looked up expectantly at our teacher, she would nod in approval and we all trooped out to watch the precision flying overhead. When Germany signed the terms for unconditional surrender, the director of our school came to announce it in person, and dismissed school for the day. Everyone was jubilant.

Some time passed before our little community transitioned to peace. Servicemen and women didn't return overnight, some returned changed, and some did not return at all. One summer day in 1945 some of my siblings and I went to town with my mother. When we returned, my father came running down the drive to meet us. He grabbed the door handle and ran along side the car, laughing as he ran. My mother assumed he was up to some nonsense and was annoyed with him, but then he opened the door and exulted, "Bob is on the way home!" The mailman had returned a letter she'd mailed to Bob, and he was indeed returning from the war.

I don't remember how much time passed before he came home, but I do remember meeting his train in Ocheyedan and seeing him smile as he walked toward us. I was six years old when he left and nearing my eleventh birthday when he returned.

Bonnie had already been discharged and was about to give birth to my first nephew. Arnold didn't receive his discharge until after we entered the nuclear age and the Japanese surrendered unconditionally.

The world was changed and the little town of Ocheyedan celebrated. Most of the soldiers from Europe were home and they reveled most of all. I was awed by the parades, ceremonies, and dancing. My mother's private ceremony was to take the flags from the window and put them away with joy and relief.

A few months later Arnold and Bonnie came home. They brought my first nephew with them. Life was good, Depression days were over, rationing was over, the war was behind us, it seemed peace would last forever, and I was the only one in my grade who was an aunt.

*Recently discovered excerpt from a letter my father wrote in 1943:
Lena is putting in almost full time on making quilts, bedroom slippers, lap robes, hats, handkerchiefs and what not for our veterans. She is chairman of our unit of Service Women of America. She has just about worn out the telephone and the rug. She gets so many calls.

Ghosts of Christmases Past

Lavish Christmas gifts were never a part of my childhood. My parents encouraged us to keep the gift of the Christ child uppermost in our hearts and not to expect a lot of material things. That was true to their core values and convictions, but I suspect they were also influenced by Depression years with little money to spend on frivolous things. I don't recall being reminded to pick up my toys, and if I had been so directed, it would not have taken long.

My mother or older sister, Marge, would always sew a new dress for me, something to wear to the children's Christmas service. Maybe there would be a pair of shoes, but only if I really needed them, or perhaps a doll with a composition head and pretty face, one I had seen in the Montgomery Ward catalog, but never bonded to. I would have preferred a gun and holster set, or if I had to have a doll I would have liked a rubber one that would take a bottle and wet its pants.

Our rural school and Sunday school provided us with brown bags containing hard candy, nuts, an apple, an orange, and the favorite part of the mix; one large chocolate drop. From gift exchanges I amassed such treasures as paper dolls, coloring books, watercolors, and sewing cards. Those cards provided me with hours of hand sewing around pictures and mottoes, using a large needle and colorful embroidery floss.

Those mottoes encouraged me to TRUST AND OBEY, WATCH AND PRAY, and many other axioms chosen to shape and refine my character. The card I liked best took the most time and gave me the following admonition: GIVE THE WORLD THE BEST YOU HAVE, AND THE BEST WILL COME BACK TO YOU. Those cards have long since met some receptive trashcan, but their short bits of wisdom continue to bounce around in my consciousness, reminders of values I still hold dear.

I lost my mother in 1964 and my father in 1973, but around Christmas in 2009 I received their best gift ever, one that had been resting in a box for most of the past forty-five years. Fitting with their ideas of good work ethics, it is a gift that requires a lot of effort on my part to bring out its value.

From 1938 until 1968 my father's family wrote letters in a round robin. Eleven siblings sent continuous messages from one home to another. Each letter was written on small three-ring binder paper for consistency and ease in mailing. When Dad received an updated grouping he removed his old letter and filed it in a notebook. Then he, often my mother, and at times my sister, Marge, wrote a new letter, placed it with the others in an envelope to be passed on to the next person on the list.

Once my sisters and I took that collected treasure with us when we visited my brother and his family in California. We spent many hours laughing, crying, and reminiscing as we enjoyed reading things written in our parents' familiar handwriting.

Occasionally I fancied the idea of typing them and running copies for all of their children, grandchildren, and future generations. But the 300 sheets with script on both sides made the task extremely daunting. With passing years conveniences became available, causing me to rethink the idea of putting the letters and some treasured family pictures into a book. Computers with word processors, email, and a recent friendship with a local publisher began to make the idea a genuine possibility.

At a reunion in May of 2009, several family members discussed methods of working toward that goal. To avoid the danger of losing some of the originals, we decided it best to make copies and send them on to various willing typists. I put out a mass email to nieces and nephews requesting volunteers. Eight came forward, including my sister, nieces, nephews, and myself. Others commented that they were poor typists, but would be glad to proofread.

The next thing was to get someone to do the copying. Six hundred fragile pages needed to be hand fed through a copying machine before going out to various places in Iowa, South Dakota, Missouri, and California. A local newspaper agreed to make the copies, but it is a tedious task, which they gave out in two sections several weeks apart. The final third lay locked away until they could find more time in January of 2010.

Not having them all at once was advantageous. It gave us time through mass emails to work out a format we could agree on. As each volunteer worked on an average of eight letters, four to six pages in length, we discussed font, indentations, footnoting, and bracketing. Probably the greatest decision was whether or not to correct spelling and other errors. After a bit of discussion and research we agreed to type the letters just as they were written. My initial thought was to make the corrections, but in retrospect,

I'm glad we opted to leave things as they were written. It brings out the character of the writers.

In a box of things my parents saved, we found charts identifying relationships and locations of Dad's siblings and descendents in the 1940s. In addition, the box contained a reminiscence essay Dad wrote in college in 1916 and a letter he sent to our mother that same year when they were dating. We also found three letters our grandmother wrote to Dad in 1910 and 1911, plus a poem she penned in German in 1881. We had Grandmother's poem translated and put into English verse—all treasures to add to the book.

When we finished typing, organizing, and filing, we gathered pictures and put it all together to be published by Jean Tennant, owner of Shapato Publishing of Everly, Iowa. Having the book professionally published will make it available online, so if we don't order enough copies at the outset, family members and interested friends can purchase it on line. This should all be finished by Christmas of 2010. In honor of my parents' belief in donating to their church and other causes, the profits realized from the sale of the books will be used as a donation in their memory to one of their favorite charities.

For those of us who remember my parents, the letters enrich our recollections and give us a chance to revisit family history, while the perspective of time enlightens our perceptions. For descendents who never knew them, the collection offers an opportunity to learn about the remarkable people I called Mom and Dad, while their faith, roots, and values touch further generations.

Thanks, Mom and Dad. Your words still influence and guide the lives of many. This legacy far exceeds the value of the holster set and rubber doll I never received. You did follow the maxim to "give the world the best you have," and your enduring faith and constant witness continue to bless our lives.

Generations That Hold the Future

My own three children, Steven Peters, Teri Gruenig, and Robert Taylor have enriched my life in many ways. The best of the many gifts they have given me are six grandchildren. Each is unique and each holds a special place in my life.

Teri's son, Jarrod Fredericks, is the oldest. Jarrod is a storyteller with a passion for hunting and fishing. He is a hard worker who was willing to take on any job to make some money while in high school and in college. He graduated from college with a business major in 2009, is gainfully employed but still thinking about other job options.

His brother, Lucas Fredericks, is the tallest of the boys, at 6'3." Unlike his brothers and cousins, hunting and fishing are not important passions. He grew up watching the History and Discovery channels, or losing himself in books. As a senior at the University of Minnesota in pre-med, he spent one semester at the University of Linkoping in Sweden. He is making decisions about what direction he'll follow next year.

Third in line is Steve and Judy's son, Brandon, who is a junior at Iowa State University, pursuing aeronautical engineering. In addition to hunting and fishing, Brandon likes water and snow boarding, skydiving and working on various unique constructions.

Teri's third son, Zachary Fredericks, is still thinking about his future. He also loves the out-of-doors and is interested in a possible career in some area of mechanics. I always thought he should become a locksmith, as his favorite things to play with as a child were keys and padlocks. He liked haunting antique shops with me, even as a preschooler.

Brandon's brother, Derek Peters, is a senior in high school, a good student, and an astute observer of all things having to do with nature, mechanics, and computers. He will follow Brandon to Iowa State and pursue some area of engineering. We will miss calling on his expertise in fixing things when he is off to college.

After having five rambunctious grandsons—who are actually men now—Robert and Missy gave us the gift of a granddaughter, Reese Taylor. Reese was born in 2007, and has become our main form of entertainment at family gatherings. She could count past twenty before she was two, has a strong vocabulary as well as a strong mind and a winning personality.

I have told zillions of stories about each of the six, and am often reminded that I should write them down. I have not done nearly enough of that, but I am including one story in this anthology about an experience I had with Brandon.

Exploring with Brandon

The morning was chilly, but my four-year-old grandson, Brandon, and I went exploring. We chose a favorite place, along the railroad tracks.

When we arrived he announced, "If you walk on the railroad tracks you have to know the rules."

"And what are the rules?" I asked.

His reply was quick and definite. "If a train comes get off the tracks."

Feeling very grown up compared to his one-year-old brother he added, "Derek doesn't know the rules so he can't walk on the railroad tracks."

Brandon carried a small blue and yellow plastic telescope to enrich his explorations. He called it his scope-looker. It was too difficult to focus the regular way so he turned it around and saw the world in a smaller perspective, more suited to his own size.

He picked up a spike that was lying on the ties. Later he found a large railroad bolt. He picked that up too, and used it for a microphone. The chill of the morning seemed to disappear and we took turns using the bolt while we sang *Itsy-Bitsy Spider* and *I'm a Little Teapot*.

As we continued we stopped to see things *micro-fied* through his scope-looker. We studied rocks, animal tracks, and ground cherries. We tasted the ground cherries and Brandon announced that they were YUCK. Later we found a bush covered with tiny black berries. I examined them carefully, but I could not identify them.

"We won't taste these," I advised Brandon. "We never eat wild berries unless we know what they are. They could be poison."

Brandon listened quietly and then he said, "I'll check them with my scope-looker."

He stood back, focused his telescope, observed the small berries, even smaller now in his view, and offered a carefully considered opinion, "Yep, poison!"

**A Time
for Peace**

Road of Recollections
Haibun*

childhood paths taken
years of innocent musings
serene recollections

The road that divided our farm from the neighbor's was little used. Little used, that is, to cars and trucks, but to the children of the neighborhood, it was a special place. The ditches were slight indentations, which filled quickly with snow in winter, allowing drifts to cover the road. Snowplows seldom ventured there, as the road was not considered important enough to open. Cars didn't venture there either, so we children rode sleds, toboggans, and scoop shovels down its beckoning hills.

The spring thaw and rains turned the road into gumbo, keeping it impassable for a time. Then we made mud pies and baked them on rocks in the sun. Summer and fall were the best times. The dried road became as smooth as pavement, a perfect place for running races or riding our bikes. The shallow ditches provided refuge for small animals and birds. We learned to recognize the songs of robins, bluebirds, meadowlarks, bob-whites, and wrens. We caught butterflies with cupped hands and let them go.

peace interrupted
familiar sound—yet surprising
a whirring of wings

Occasionally we were startled when an equally startled ring-necked pheasant flushed from one of the ditches. If we were lucky, we might happen upon a nest of fluffy striped pheasant chicks. Though the temptation was great, we wouldn't touch them. Someone had told us that if we did, the mothers wouldn't come near the chicks again. We firmly believed that was true.

Squirrels, rabbits, and field mice would hop and scamper into view. There were badger holes in the ground and woodpecker holes in the trees, as well as raccoon tracks that looked like babies' handprints.

evidence whispers
of wonders—mysterious
almost unheeded

At times the faint, musky odor of a skunk hung over the countryside. We knew that a village of nocturnal inhabitants lived beneath our feet. That thought, along with the sight of an occasional garter snake, stirred a strange uneasiness within me.

Among the wildflowers, asparagus grew in profusion. We learned all of the best spots to find it among the prairie grasses. It was important to harvest it before it grew tall and woody, or went to seed. The taste and texture were just right for cooking and canning when the stalks were four to eight inches high.

The essence of the white plum blossoms promised a harvest of tangy plums to be preserved in the fall. We watched the choke-cherries all season and delighted to see them turn red. They coated our tongues with a fascinating bitterness.

> *nature's refinement*
> *profusion of colors*
> *announce the new seasons*

Flowers bloomed from spring to fall. Violets and dandelions emerged first. Then came the sorrel with a sourness that intrigued us as much as the chokecherries. Summer brought bouncing Bet, red and yellow clover, four o'clocks, and daylilies. Soon we found sectioned scouring rush, which we called snake grass. We patiently picked the stems and sectioned them to-gether, constructing circles, triangles, squares, or make-believe railroad tracks, which crossed the road. As fall approached, the ditches blossomed with goldenrod, black-eyed Susans, and purple coneflowers. Then leaves turned to reds, yellows, and browns, giving notice that soon the snow would fall again.

> *musings of childhood*
> *recollections now golden*
> *smooth roadbeds of age*

The wildflowers, birds, and butterflies filled my childhood with all the color and beauty of a prairie sunset. As the sun in the evening slips from view, my road has slipped from my life. Yet the simple beauties dawn frequently upon my consciousness, evoking memories to lighten life's darkest moments.

*Haibun was originally a Japanese form of writing, a combination of prose and haiku poetry. Haiku, a form of poetry with seventeen or fewer syllables, is an insight into a moment of experience, and a haibun is the story or narrative of how one came to have that experience.

Glacial Deposits in Iowa Soil
Haiku Sequence

wonders of childhood
stones in flowing creek waters
splashes of joy

rocky reminders
ice-age glacial deposits
dot Iowa fields

shrouded truths surface
ground and smoothed by time's passage
the heart's stony soil

gatherers, hunters
souvenirs of a past time
to nurture our souls

concepts refuted
past discernments discarded
misgivings unmasked

memories of childhood
like stones settling in creek beds
eroded, refined

The Amber Season

The seasons come and go in succession. Hues and colors seem appropriate according to those seasons. I have a string of amber beads that I wear whenever it pleases me, but they are most appropriate in the fall. The beads are not perfectly shaped ovals or spheres, but nuggets shaped by natural events. Their amber color, which fits the shades of the countryside, now seems to symbolize the autumn of my life.

In a time past remembering, those nuggets were conceived in the heartwood of young pine trees in northern Europe, then permeated with tree oils and *resin-ated* from the sapwood. In some ancient era the trees decayed, became buried under the earth or rotted under water. During this process the resin fossilized into amber.

The Baltic Sea often washes this treasure to the shore, or fishermen find it in their nets. Miners nearby collect it from blue earth. Craftsmen shape some pieces into jewelry, parts of small boxes, mouthpieces for pipes, or other decorations. They send the less desirable pieces on to be used in varnishes or chemicals.

The nuggets tell their stories. Some carry fossilized scars from contact with sand, stone, or rotted bark. Some reflect a colorful past, others seem to have led a rather bland life, but most reflect a mixture of experiences. An occasional insect might be embedded in the amber.*

I sometimes wonder whether the insect was attracted to the resin, or the resin to the insect. Perhaps the alliance came from a mutual agreement. Now the nuggets carry evidence of an ongoing commitment or perhaps a trap.

In my Amber Season I am aware that I am spelling out my life's story by my merits or lack of them. Still, I trust that my amber will be washed freely to the shore. Then left in its natural form, not manipulated by human hands or ingenuity, it will bear evidence that in spite of imperfections, it was shaped by the Master's hand.

*en.wikipedia.org/wiki/Amber
archaeology.about.com/od/baterms/qu/baltic-amber.htm

Some of the essays and poems within have appeared in previous publications:

The Hartley *Sentinel*:
> "In the Company of Losers." January 2009
> "Remembering the Waterbed." February 2009
> "A Glitch in Time." July 2009
> "Going into Overtime." August 2009
> "Dream Vacation, 2001." September 2009
> "Of Genealogy and Outhouses." October 2009
> "Exploring with Brandon." November 2009
> "A Word to the Wise." April 2010

Julien's Journal
> "Love in the Woods." February 2009
> "Grandma's Living Legacy." May 2009
> "Reorientation." September 2009
> "Life and Death Connections." October 2009
> "A Glitch in Time," June 2010
> "Land Between Two Rivers," July 2010

Lyrical Iowa
> "Final Performance." 1969
> "Collections." 2002
> "Sonnet to a Prairie Rose." 2003
> "Mother's Oblations." 2004
> "Moonlight Madness." 2008
> "Land Between Two Rivers." 2009

Northwest Iowa Review
> "Road of Recollections." September 2007

Walking Beans Wasn't Something You Did With Your Dog
> "Stars in the Window." November 2008

www.ingramcontent.com/pod-product-compliance
Lightning Source LLC
Chambersburg PA
CBHW050825180626
46814CB00004B/1457